Steve Morse:

MELODIC**ROCK** GUITAR**CONCEPTS**

Master Melodic Rock Soloing with the Dixie Dregs & Deep Purple Guitar Virtuoso

STEVE**MORSE**

FUNDAMENTAL**CHANGES**

Steve Morse: Melodic Rock Guitar Concepts

Master Melodic Rock Soloing with the Dixie Dregs & Deep Purple Guitar Virtuoso

ISBN: 978-1-78933-252-0

Published by **www.fundamental-changes.com**

Copyright © 2023 Steve Morse

Edited by Tim Pettingale

www.fundamental-changes.com

Over 12,000 fans on Facebook: **FundamentalChangesInGuitar**

Instagram: **FundamentalChanges**

For over 350 Free Guitar Lessons with Videos Check Out

www.fundamental-changes.com

Cover Image Copyright: Author photo, used by permission

Special thanks to Pete Sklaroff for his assistance with this project.

https://musicservices.petesklaroff.com/

Contents

Introduction

When I look back at some of my favorite guitar players over the years, I can see a common thread in their playing. It's something that really appeals to me, both as a listener and a guitar player, and that is *melodic phrasing*.

Eric Clapton has great feel and a natural instinct for creating melodic phrases. Jeff Beck's phrasing is immaculate, coupled with his sense of adventure and musical exploration. I always feel that you can almost hear Joe Walsh breathe between his phrases, because each musical idea he expresses is so well formed. George Harrison never wasted a note and always played something perfectly fitting for the song. Steve Howe showed me that it was fine to fuse together different styles to create interesting melodic phrases – in his case, classical and rock. And Jimmy Page's ability with melodic phrasing is expressed through the many memorable riffs he composed, as well as his solos.

Great phrasing is important because it enables us to tell a story with our music. All of the great players I've mentioned are also great *storytellers*. When they play a solo, it has a clear beginning, middle and end; it has purpose and direction; it creates a certain vibe or evokes a specific emotion. All of these things are the *why* of melodic phrasing. Here we are going to work on the *how*.

It's been said before, but the plectrum doesn't need to take a breath, so guitarists are often guilty of overplaying. Horn players are forced to think in phrases because they *have* to take a breath. Guitar players don't have that constraint, so if we want to develop the art of playing strong, melodic phrases that connect with our audiences, we need to employ some deliberate strategies.

In this book we'll explore my rock guitar vocabulary and I'll show you some of the strategies I use to create strong phrases. We'll do so over tracks that have a major, minor and dominant focus, so you can understand the scales and melodic ideas I use in a variety of musical settings. Then we'll look at the important idea of creating tension and resolution in your solos, for when you want to push the harmonic envelope a bit further.

Let's go!

Steve

Chapter One – Dominant-Focus Melodic Phrasing

In this chapter, the track we are working with is played in the key of G Major. The G chord that drives the tune, however, has a dominant chord (G7) feel, so when it comes to scale choices, we'll use G Mixolydian as well as Major/Minor Pentatonic and Blues scale ideas. I'll show you how I combine these sounds into a single hybrid scale.

You'll hear that the main riff is played with the classic "Bo Diddley" rhythm. This is a slightly altered version of the Latin 3-2 clave rhythm and shows how Bo adapted the Afro-Cuban groove to play it in a Rock 'n' Roll setting. The tune has a middle eight or B section that has a slight Celtic influence, in contrast to the main riff.

First, let's take a brief look at the rhythm guitar parts before we move on to the solo.

The Rhythm Part

The main riff consists of simple power chords. A G5 chord briefly moves down to F5 and back, but it's clear that the main tonal center is G.

The riff is played as a 1/16th note strumming pattern. To capture the authentic Bo Diddley feel, it's important to control the muted accents and make the main chord accents pop out. The best way to do this, especially when using an overdriven tone, is by using a combination of picking hand palm mutes and fretting hand mutes.

Rest the fleshy part of the picking hand near to the saddle of the guitar to apply and control the palm mutes. With the fretting hand, lightly release the pressure on the strings to play each muted accent. This combination approach should produce the desired result.

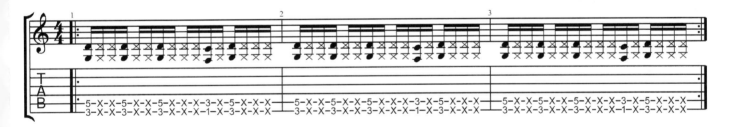

In the introduction section to the tune, over the main riff I play a complementary riff idea. This figure is an F5 chord sliding into G5. These mini-chords are voiced two octaves above the main rhythm riff, so that sonically there is still plenty of space in the music.

Let's look briefly at the eight bars of the B section, which occur twice during the tune.

Here we move into the key of F Major. An Am (chord iii in the key of F Major), leads to Bb (chord IV), F (chord I) and then C (chord V), where the Bo Diddley rhythm is repeated.

In bar five, the harmony begins to transition back to its G tonal center. Here, the C chord functions as chord IV in the key of G Major, G/B is an inversion of G major, and the Am is chord ii.

The G# bass note of the Am/G# chord is a passing note intended to connect the A note to the G key center. Before we return to the G riff, however, we have two bars of D7 (chord V of G Major), which also wants to resolve to G. Because the G# and D bass notes are a flat five interval apart, this movement provides some brief dissonance as the tune turns around.

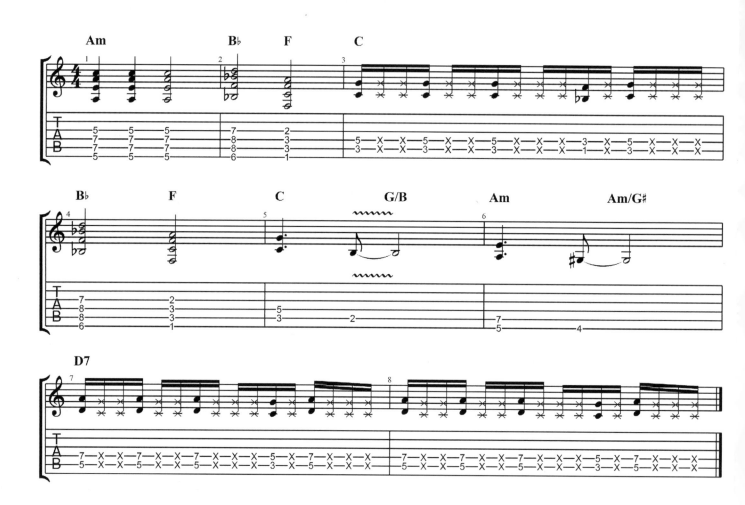

Now let's look at some of the phrasing ideas used in the solo.

It's important to preface this section by saying that, when I solo, I don't often plan what I'm going to play. At its heart, soloing is improvisation. While it might be sensible to plan out a solo for a recording session, often the best solos emerge when we are in the moment, thinking about the vibe of the tune and the emotion we want to convey. The last thing on our mind should be what notes or scales we are going to play.

However, if we want to achieve improvisational freedom, we first need to have in place some solid phrasing strategies to fall back on.

First, a word about listening to your own playing…

There is no doubt that the best way to get better at soloing is by doing it. Playing a lot is important, of course, but so is listening back to what you do.

Some guitar players have no idea how they sound because they've never listened to themselves. If you record yourself and listen back, things will nearly always jump out at you and you'll probably say, "Why do I do *that* all the time?!" Often, we are unaware of idiosyncrasies in our playing. Recording can be a vulnerable process that shows up the good, the bad and the ugly, but it's a great way to reveal and quickly fix aspects of your playing that you don't like.

Bearing this advice in mind, let's look at some simple strategies you can use to begin to improve your phrasing. The more you practice and use these techniques, the more natural they'll become and the less you'll have to think about them.

Solo Breakdown

My first tip for constructing any solo is to begin with a strong opening statement. Bars 1-2 start the solo with a G Blues scale lick. Although it sounds like a simple idea, after the opening upward bend there is a tricky string change that requires rolling your finger from the B to G string to execute the downward, half step bend.

The rest of the phrase runs down the Blues scale to end with an inflection bend that pushes the minor 3rd note into a major 3rd (Bb to B).

If you're going to play a straightforward blues lick, then pack it with as much emotion as you can. Notice on the audio download that I use a fast, wide vibrato to emphasize the bends.

Example 1a

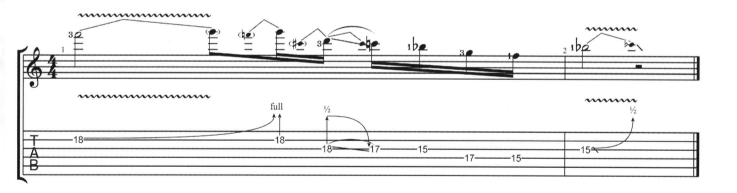

A large part of blues and rock guitar phrasing uses a *question and answer* approach to form melodic ideas. This is one of the easiest and most musical ways to discipline yourself to play succinct melodic phrases.

Compare the licks in examples 1a and 1b and you'll hear that the first is the question and the second is the answer. Question and answer phrases are often rhythmically similar, but don't have to have identical notes. Often, the question phrase is played in the higher register and the answer in the lower register, or vice versa. Together they form a complete musical idea.

Country guitar has always been a huge influence on my style, and in Example 1b I play a country style double-stop lick. It mimics the sound of a pedal steel guitar and turns a Gsus2 chord into G major.

Notice how this pattern visually fits around the E Minor Pentatonic box shape in twelfth position. This lick can be used equally well over an E minor chord, creating a minor 7 sound. Stevie Ray Vaughn used this idea a lot in his playing.

Example 1b

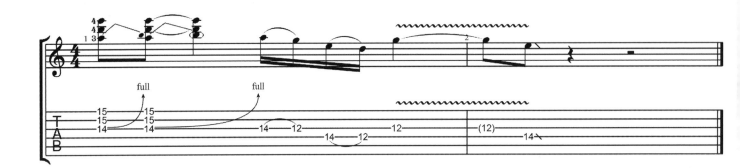

Bars 1-2 of Example 1c have another country idea repurposed for rock. This is a pedal tone lick. The G note on the high E string, fret 15 is the pedal tone, while the bends on the B string play a descending line.

The 1/16th note run in bars 3-4 uses the G Mixolydian scale, but with added chromatic passing tones. First try out the lick, then I'll expand on the idea of embellishing the Mixolydian scale.

Example 1c

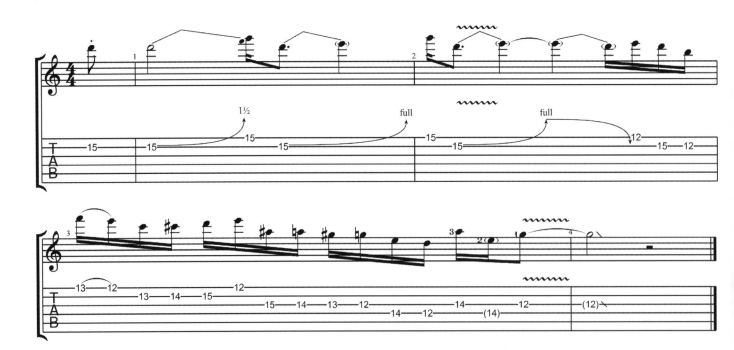

There are many ways to interpret lines that contain passing notes. For me, this idea was inspired by the jazz saxophonists I've listened to in the past, but especially Charlie Parker. Parker had a way of dancing around the chord tones of an arpeggio and could very easily move *outside* and back *inside* the harmony using chromatic approach notes.

Over dominant chords, Parker would spell out the chord tones by embellishing them with notes a half step above or below. It became the heart of the bebop sound, but we can take this idea and apply it in a rock guitar setting to create moments of dissonance which are then resolved. It's a sound has always appealed to me.

When playing over a dominant chord vamp, I'll often use an enhanced Mixolydian scale that includes some chromatic notes. You may have heard the term Mixolydian Blues scale used, which is essentially what this is. As easy way to think about it is a Mixolydian scale that has borrowed some notes from the Blues scale.

The table below shows the notes/intervals of G Mixolydian:

G	A	B	C	D	E	F
Root	2	3	4	5	6	b7

The G Blues scale has the following notes/intervals:

G	Bb	C	Db	D	F
Root	b3	4	b5	5	b7

The G Blues scale has four notes in common with G Mixolydian and two notes that are different – the b3 (Bb) and b5 (Db).

We can borrow those two notes to form the hybrid Mixolydian Blues scale – a nine-note scale with the formula 1 2 b3 3 4 b5 5 6 b7.

What's really useful about this hybrid scale is that it has both major and minor qualities (emphasizing both the major and minor 3rd is one of the key ideas of the blues), plus the dissonant b5 "blue" note.

The diagrams below illustrate the G Mixolydian Blues scale in third position, showing both the notes and the relationship of the intervals to the root.

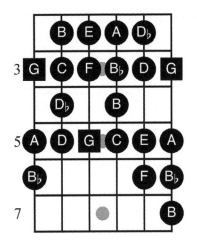
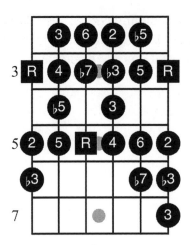

Experiment with this scale and listen to how it sounds over a G dominant chord. You can use the backing track for this chapter to jam over.

The addition of chromatic notes opens an easy way to introduce tension into an otherwise plain sounding diatonic scale. First see what licks you can come up with on your own, then listen to how I add different tension notes from this scale in the lines that follow.

One of the things I like to do is to create short sequences with scales. This means ordering the notes in such a way as to avoid simply running up/down the scale. Bar 1 of Example 1d is a typical example and the result is a motif-like idea. Notice that I'm emphasizing the Bb note (b3) in this lick.

Example 1d

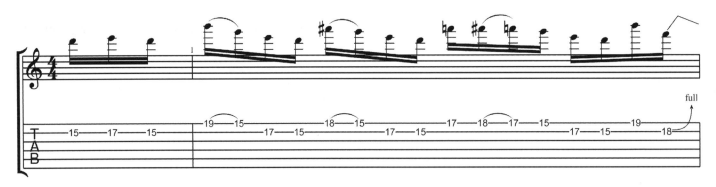

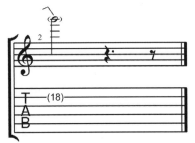

Another way of freshening up a scale is by introducing wider intervals by skipping strings. Here is an intervallic lick that skips two strings. The G note on the D string at the 17th fret acts a pedal tone against the bends on the high E string. The higher notes are descending the scale stepwise.

Executing an idea like this takes more fretting hand strength than you might think to perfectly hit the notes and hold them in pitch, so strive for accuracy when you play.

Example 1e

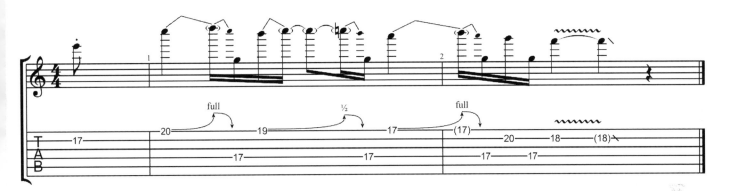

Example 1f brings together the previous three ideas.

First, it's a sequencing lick that creates a descending motif and also includes string skipping. This one will be a cross picking workout for you!

It's also a question and answer phrase. Although the "answer" in bars 3-4 doesn't repeat the sequence idea of bars 1-2, it has enough rhythmic similarity to make the two parts fit together as a complete idea.

The third idea is relatively simple one – a descending melody that is embellished – but it's all about smooth execution. Again, we're using the Mixolydian Blues scale to introduce the tension notes.

Example 1f

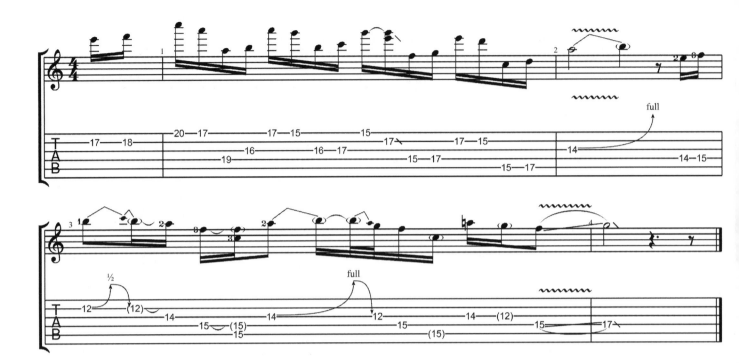

Now we reach the B section of the tune. For this middle section, instead of blowing over the changes I decided to play a pre-composed melody that outlined the harmony. Whenever we take a solo, what we play has to be fitting for the piece. It's easy to play familiar licks and just blow over the changes, but will that serve the song?

Here, the harmony of the B section is well defined, compared to the free-flowing dominant vamp either side of it, so it made sense to play something which highlighted that contrast.

Example 1g

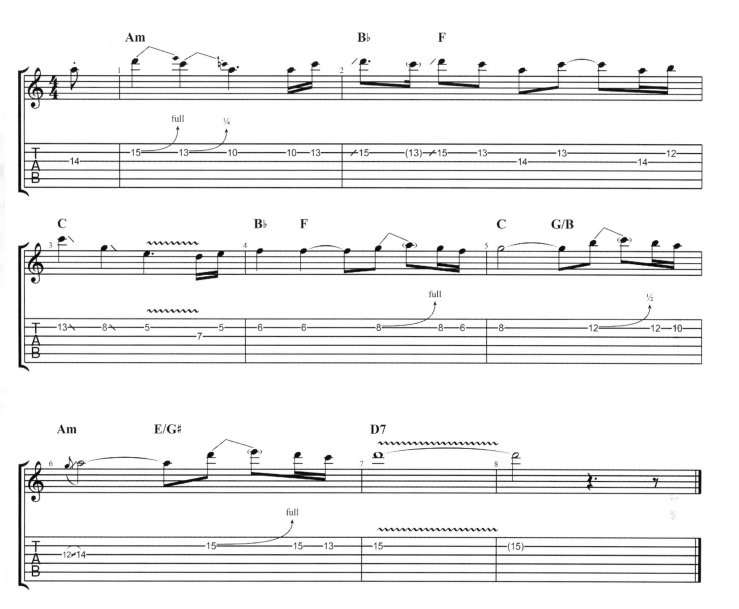

Now we are back to the Bo Diddley vamp. Over the next two examples, we are going to explore some new phrasing ideas: *use of space,* giving your lines *momentum and direction*, and *rhythmic diversity.*

When starting a solo, it's tempting to go in all guns blazing, but we shouldn't be afraid of using space. What we leave out is as important as what we put in. In bars 1-2, I hold onto the bends and allow the notes to sustain over the groove.

This paves the way for the faster lick that spans bars 3-4. Here, an idea begins that continues in Example 1i. It's all about forward momentum and here the lines are more scalic. This is an example of what you could call *harmonic targeting.* In other words, I have in mind a bent note that I'm aiming for and the ascending scale runs are a way of getting me to that destination.

Example 1h

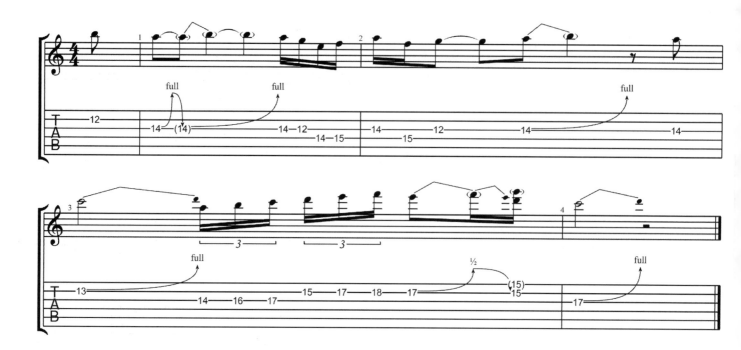

The targeting idea continues in the pickup bar and bar one of Example 1i.

For the remainder of this lick, I focus on mixing up the rhythms to create a new point of interest. We guitar players don't always make the most of the simple rhythmic devices available to us, which could make our playing so much more compelling to listen to.

Later, when you piece together these licks to play the solo as a complete piece, you'll see that many of the phrases begin on the "&" of the previous bar. Though I'm playing simple ascending scale runs, the rhythmic structure brings a point of interest and makes the lines less predictable.

One rhythmic device you can easily engage with is to play a phrase then repeat it, displacing it to begin on a different beat of the bar. Rhythmically breaking up a lick, or displacing it, changes its character and emphasis and is a very effective tool.

Notice the idea in bars 3-4 below, where I'm punching out dotted 1/8th notes. It creates a three-over-four feel that pulls against the groove and makes the line stand out.

Example 1i

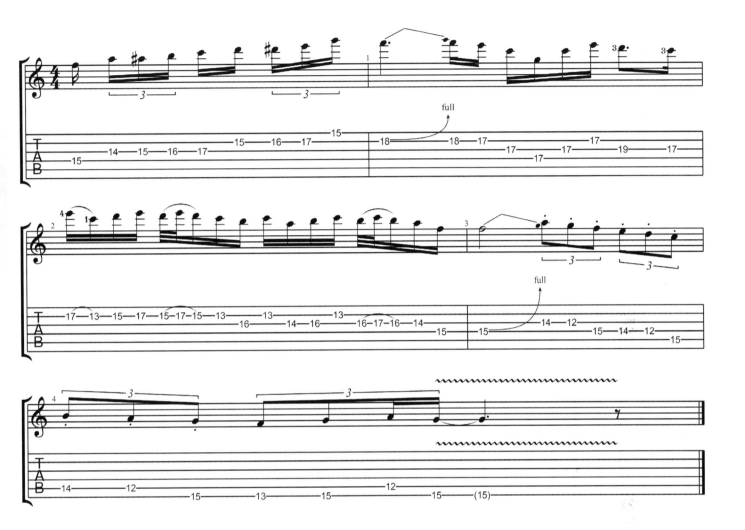

Example 1j begins with another targeted run that starts in the previous bar to add rhythmic diversity and create a line of unpredictable length.

It's worth taking some time to study the 1/16th note run that spans bars 3-4. It's the kind of idea I like to play that combines both my country and bebop influences. It has an undeniable country "sound" but is bebop-like in its execution. Like a Charlie Parker lick, it dances around the strong scale tones, using chromatic approach notes.

Unlike bebop, however – where the aim is usually to play chord/scale tones on the strong beats of the bar and chromatic notes on the off beats – I'm happy to include more dissonance and allow some of the passing notes to land on the down beat. It works because the line has a strong sense of *momentum and direction*, which carries the listener to the end destination.

Example 1j

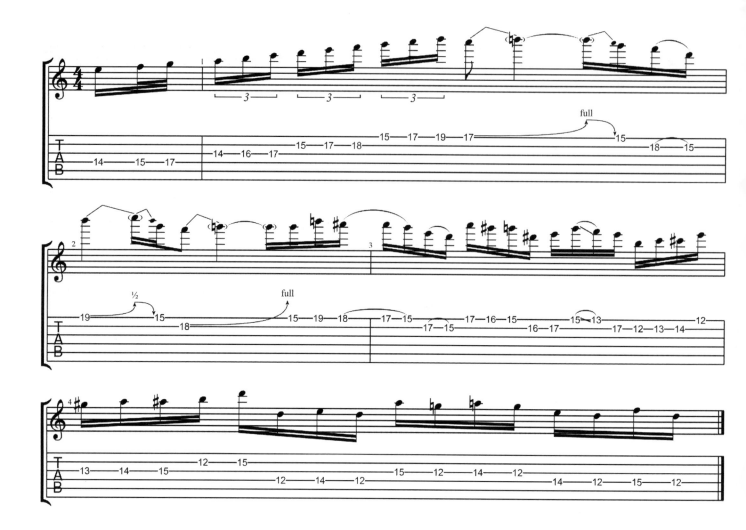

The final lick of the solo is another question and answer idea. Really, it's a question that is answered twice, the last time down an octave, but I introduce more rhythmic variation to disguise it.

Example 1k

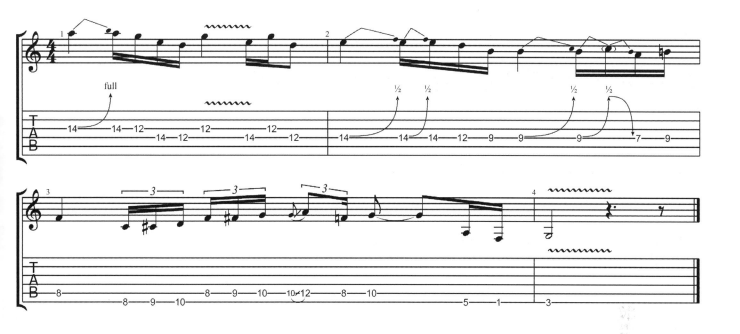

Next comes a repeat of the B section of the tune, where we play the pre-written melody learnt earlier. On the recording you'll hear that I play a harmony part to give this section a lift.

This is followed by a lick that will end the tune. Closing statements are as important as opening statements. Just as a lick needs to have a clear beginning, middle and end, so does your entire solo.

I decided to end with a motif-based idea that targets G Mixolydian scale notes, playing a short phrase with passing notes before each one.

Example 1l

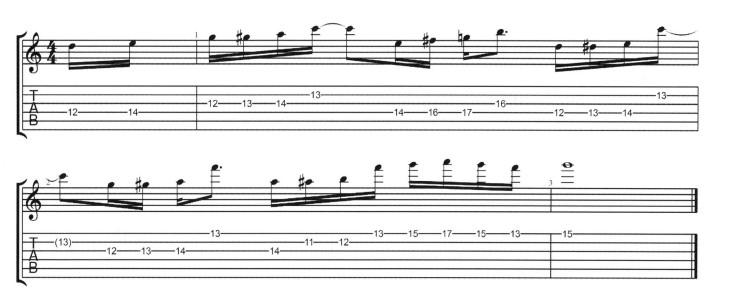

Before you tackle the solo in full, here is a reminder of the melodic phrasing ideas we've discussed in this chapter.

- *Question and answer phrases.* Consider breaking up your phrases and connecting them with call and response ideas to keep them cohesive

- *Complete ideas.* Make sure your phrases have a clear beginning, middle and end

- *Sequencing.* Work at developing sequencing ideas for scales, so that you don't play the notes in a predictable order

- *Passing notes.* Use chromatic passing notes to add tension to otherwise diatonic sounding scales and experiment with the Mixolydian Blues scale

- *Targeting a destination.* Give your phrases momentum and direction by having a destination in mind

- *Rhythmic devices.* Introduce rhythmic diversity, repeating phrases on different beats of the bar

- *Contrast.* Use contrast to add movement to your solo (slow versus fast; soulful versus intense; held bends versus scale runs, etc.)

- *Space.* Use space and think about how what is *not* played affects the piece. Placing limits on ourselves often stimulates creativity. If we discipline ourselves to play shorter phrases, for instance, as opposed to long runs, often the result is something more meaningful and melodic.

Now have a listen to the audio for Example 1m and have a go at playing the entire solo.

Example 1m

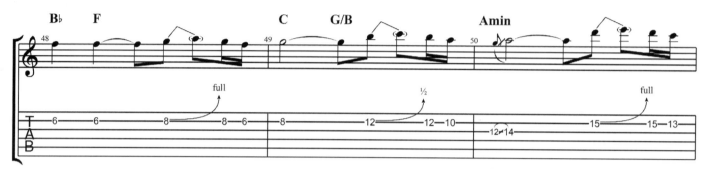

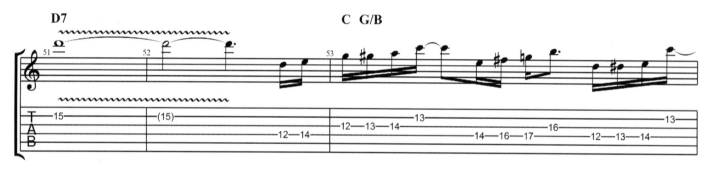

Picking Technique 101

Before we move onto some Major-focused melodic lines, if you found any of the picking in the previous solo challenging, it may be worth your while to spend some time drilling your technique. Even if you feel you're a competent picker, it's always useful to assess where you're at by being forced to play something you wouldn't normally play. Being good at playing something we know inside out can often mask where we're really at, technically.

In this brief workshop you'll find a series of exercises to help you drill your picking technique, so you'll be better prepared to tackle fast sequenced runs and cross-picked passages. After the drills, you'll find an example of how you might turn an exercise into a melodic line, but you should experiment with all the drills and find ways to incorporate these ideas into your rock vocabulary.

Advice on picking mechanics

First, a word about the picking technique that I use. Everyone has their own, slightly different take on picking technique, but I'll explain my approach.

I grip the pick between the thumb and first finger. The thumb is in the center of the pick, so that a small triangle of plectrum is available to connect with the strings. Assuming you have a regular sized pick, the top curve of the pick will be slightly visible above the thumb and not concealed by it.

I begin by positioning my picking hand so that the pick sits at a perfect 90-degree right angle to the strings. Everything I pick is strictly alternate picked with a continuous *down-up* movement. With my second and third fingers curled inward to the palm of the hand, I allow my pinkie finger to float around the bottom of the strings, often resting on the bottom of the high E string.

This serves two purposes: first, as I move my hand across the strings to pick a passage, say from the high E string to the low E string, the pinkie provides some muting for the strings that I don't want to ring out. Secondly, it provides a kind of anchor for the picking hand and helps to maintain the correct picking angle and distance from the strings. Sometimes, I anchor the pinkie to the body of the guitar if I need extra stability when picking a very fast passage.

Finally, I rotate my wrist very slightly, back and forth, when picking. This causes the pick to angle downward, so that it doesn't hit the strings straight, but with a *downward slant.*

The purpose of this mechanic is that, when picking *downward*, less of the pick needs to connect with the string in order to sound it, and when picking *upward*, the pick can rise out of the string efficiently, without accidentally striking an adjacent string.

The very slight rotation of my wrist when picking means that my pick is swooping down on the strings in an arc rather than a straight line, and this helps solve the problem of tricky inside string changes when picking passages.

NB: There is a video of me on YouTube where I have a camera attached to my guitar and shows my picking action in slow motion. It will help to see my picking technique in practice, to understand how the mechanics come together.

Now onto the exercises. In the notation below you'll see that fingering and picking directions are included for each drill.

Let's begin with a very common exercise that has been used extensively over the years because it's an ideal warm-up routine. We are picking a chromatic four-note pattern in straight 1/8th notes across the strings in one zone of the fretboard.

After ascending from the sixth to first string, we move up one fret before descending, so we can continue an unbroken alternate picking pattern.

Begin by playing it very slowly to ensure that your picking action is working efficiently and economically. It's important to be precise with your picking before speeding up, otherwise you'll just be playing your bad habits faster.

Exercise 1

The next drill uses the exact same pattern, but this time is played using 1/8th note triplets. Because we're retaining the four notes per string pattern, it means we'll play one complete triplet and the first note of the next triplet on one string before moving to the adjacent string. Having half of the triplets arranged across two strings just takes a bit of thinking about, and the important thing is to fix the triplet sound in your mind as you play.

Exercise 2

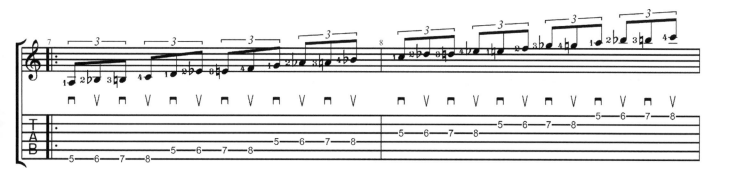

Next is a root-5th-root picking exercise designed to sharpen your picking technique across strings. Again, it's arranged in triplets, but this time it's the string changes and position shifts that can trip you up. Play it slowly to begin with and get every note sounding cleanly, then focus on smoothly shifting between the ascending and descending shapes.

Exercise 3

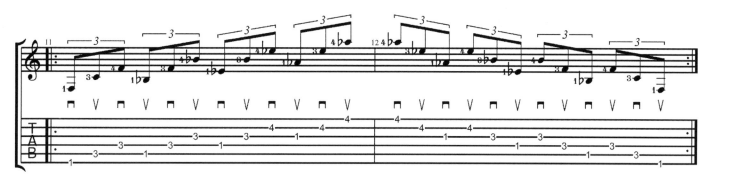

Exercise 4 is designed to help you practice skipping strings. Each phrase, launched from the bottom four strings, skips one string and moves across the neck. Aim for picking accuracy and an economical movement of the pick across the strings. Keep the pick as close to the strings as possible and don't lift it vertically away from the guitar to "jump" between them. This whole exercise works as a lick in the key of F Minor.

Exercise 4

Exercises 5, 6 and 7 all drill two-note-per-string patterns, with each one increasing the interval between the first note and the second. These are non-musical patterns designed to get you moving your picking hand quickly and efficiently across the strings, playing fewer notes per string in a single position.

Exercise 5

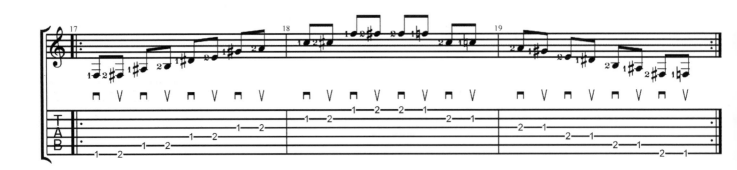

Exercise 6

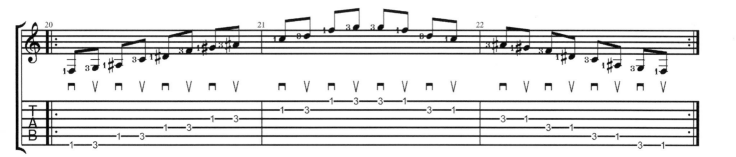

Exercise 7

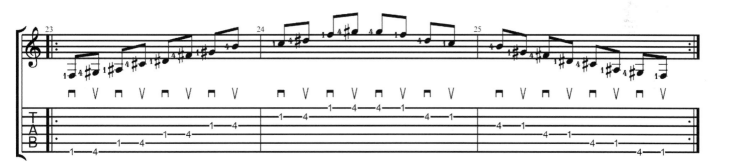

Here's another exercise that splits triplets across strings and requires one small position shift.

Exercise 8

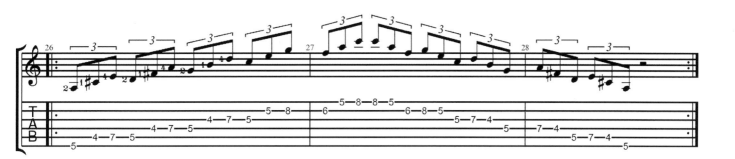

With the next exercise it's back to string skipping. We start by skipping just one string, then switch to skipping two strings. With a pivot phrase in bar five we then reverse the pattern for the descent. Again, it's not particularly musical, it's just designed to test your picking technique by getting you to play patterns you wouldn't naturally jump to.

Work with a metronome and start by playing it at an easy, slow tempo. Once you've mastered the pattern and can play it cleanly, keep increasing your metronome speed in increments of 5bpm. Keep cranking up the speed until you're at the very edge of your ability to execute the line. Make a note of the fastest comfortable tempo for you and begin close to that next time.

Exercise 9

Finally, as a challenge, here's a line that I might typically play, which relies on a number of skills taught in the previous exercises. Use your metronome and repeat the process of beginning slowly and gradually pushing to the edge of your ability. It's the process of going beyond your ability that will stretch and improve your technical skills.

Exercise 10

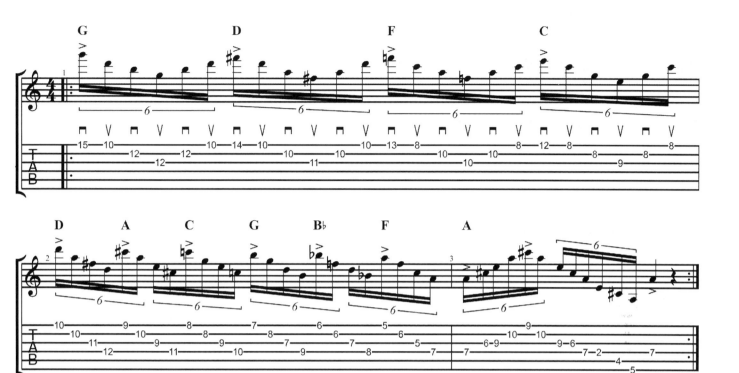

Chapter Two – Major-Focus Melodic Phrasing

About the track

In this chapter, the track we're looking at has a driving, energetic feel to it and is in the key of A Major. Have a listen to the backing track before reading on and imagine that you/your band have written this instrumental number. As the lead guitar player, you are now tasked with coming up with something interesting to embellish the track and, of course, you'll have to take a solo on it too. On listening, what sort of ideas occur to you?

When presented with something like this, I always think compositionally. In other words, I want to play something that is both melodic and memorable – like the hook of any great tune. As guitar players, it's very tempting to just play something, *anything*, that fits, so it's good to constantly check ourselves and ask, *what are we actually saying with our instrument*? Thinking like a composer will help us to make stronger statements with our melodies and will also improve our phrasing.

First, let's have a look at the rhythm part that opens the tune. It's a typical rock rhythm based around an A5 power chord. Palm muting helps to achieve the staccato rhythm and punches out the part.

Example 2a

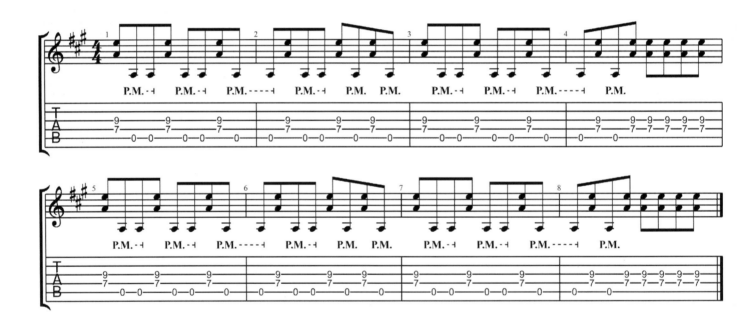

The first challenge is to come up with an opening melodic statement that works over the rhythm part. I decided to play a question and answer type phrase that has a repeating rhythmic structure. The phrase uses a string skip at the beginning to make it more interesting. Bars 1-4 are the question part of the phrase.

You might also notice that there is a question and answer embedded *within* the question phrase – the phrase in bar two is a response to bar one.

Example 2b

The answer happens in the subsequent four bars. Bar one of Example 2c is identical to bar one of the previous example, then a variation is played in bar two. Again, there is an answer within the answer.

Example 2c

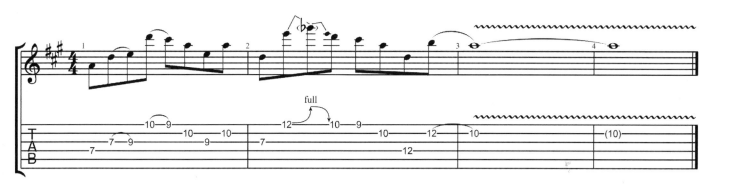

At this point, the rhythm guitar shifts to playing a different pattern, so we need a new variation of melody to play over the top. Let's look at the rhythm part first.

The new part contrasts effectively with the earlier one by shifting to palm-muted intervals in thirds. The muted thirds are a somewhat blank canvas that will allow the melody to jump out to the listener.

Also, using consistent intervals like this makes the part more integral to the composition, rather than just using, say, power chords. The dynamics are pulled back here so that they don't overpower the new melody.

Example 2d

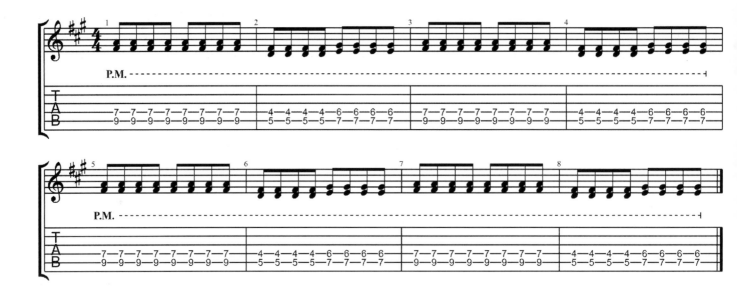

For the melodic line that sits on top, first and foremost I wanted to create a melodic statement that describes the underlying harmony, and you'll see I've taken a very thematic approach to make the melody memorable.

Rhythmically, I'm mostly keeping to 1/8th notes with added string bends to give the part a more vocal quality. The main melody is built over the first three bars, then I repeat it, call and response style.

The second repetition occurs in bars 5-7, but I changed the ending of the phrase by using a half-step bend up to the C# note in bar seven. The melody concludes using the D Major scale to descend from the C# to an octave below.

Example 2e

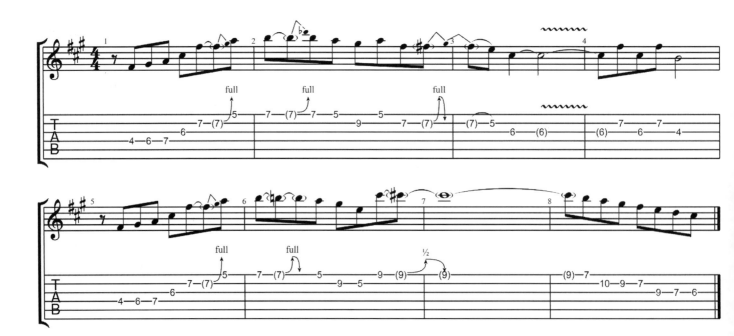

The next eight-bar section repeats the rhythm and melody line of examples 2d and 2e, so to maintain interest we add a second guitar part playing a counter melody.

To be effective compositionally, this new melody has to contrast with, but also be supportive of, the original. I've therefore chosen to play much longer note values here. I was also conscious of the rhythmic phrasing of the original melody, because we don't want to create parts that cancel each other out when played together.

You'll hear that I chose to play this new melody in a higher register to make the part distinctive and I've added some string bends throughout to complement those used in the original melody.

Example 2f

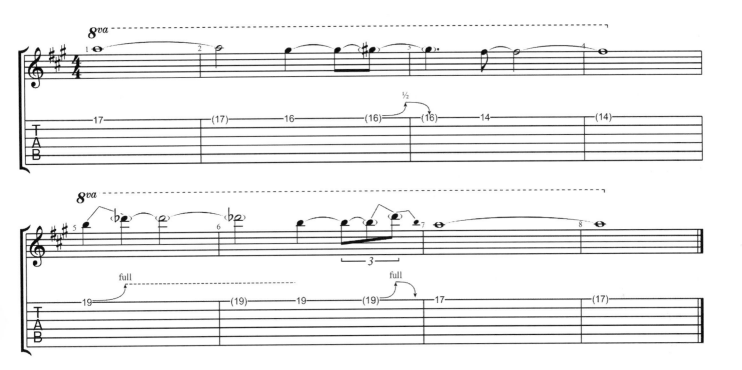

In the next eight-bar section of the tune there is a drum breakdown, the rhythm part is different, and harmony guitar parts work together to launch into the solo.

This section has a change in rhythm guitar approach. It returns to palm-muted 1/8th notes but with a different intervallic structure. Bars 1-2 are diatonic 5ths, and triads (F# minor) are heard briefly in bars 3-4.

Example 2g

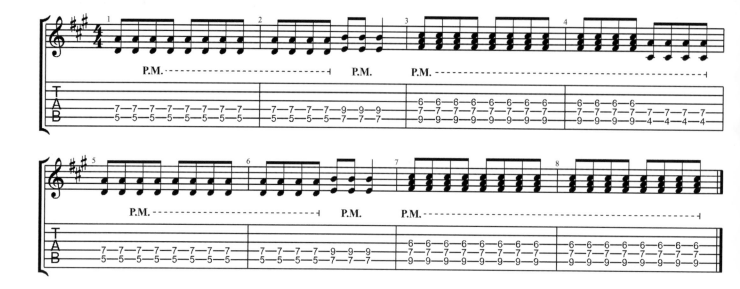

The harmonized melody is split into two distinct parts, both using diatonic intervals from the parent key of A Major. I've also chosen to play these parts in a higher register on the neck to really make them stand out in the recording.

Harmony parts like this don't have to be rhythmically identical, and if you compare Example 2h with 2i, you'll see that there is some subtle variation of rhythm between them.

Here's the first part:

Example 2h

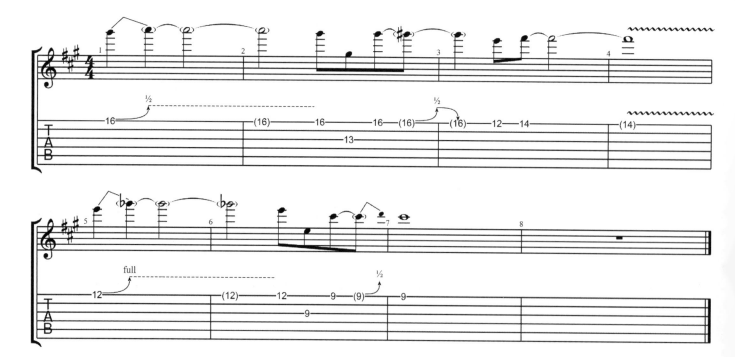

The second part of the harmonized guitar line (Example 2i) is played very high up on the fretboard and begins with a whole-step bend at the 24th fret, right at the top of the neck! You'll see that I've not simply duplicated the rhythms from the lower guitar line but made some subtle changes (e.g. using 1/4 notes in bar six against the 1/8th notes of the other guitar part).

Example 2i

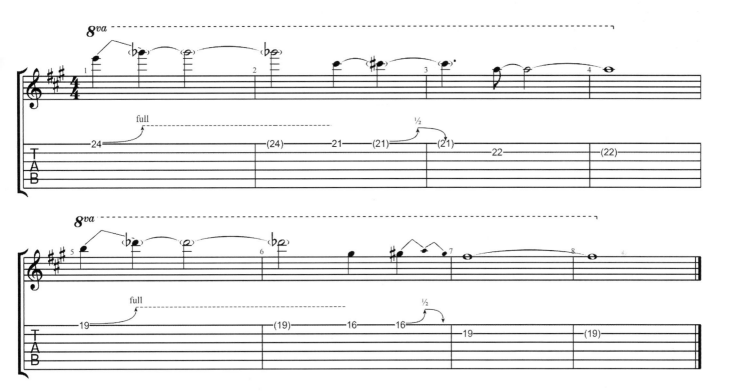

Solo Breakdown

We're now at the point in the tune where there is space for a solo. I'll break down for you in sections all the ideas that went into creating the solo, then you can play through the whole thing.

Example 2j shows a simple approach you can take to beginning a solo, where your phrases gradually build. It's tempting to set off at 100 miles an hour but, of course, that leaves you nowhere to go, and we've already noted that playing a convincing solo is like telling a story.

In this example, I begin by playing a climbing pick-up in 1/8th notes before bending the E note on the third string, fret 9, up a whole step. This sets up some effective rhythmic repetition that takes place over the next two bars.

I stay with the string bends as I ascend the scale over the next two bars. By bar 4, I'm beginning to add more subdivisions into the solo and move from 1/8th notes to 1/4 notes and triplets. I'm mostly playing diatonically at this point, keeping within the A Major/F# Minor key center.

Notice that the first few bars here are phrased around melodic motifs rather than just scale passages or pure arpeggios.

Example 2j

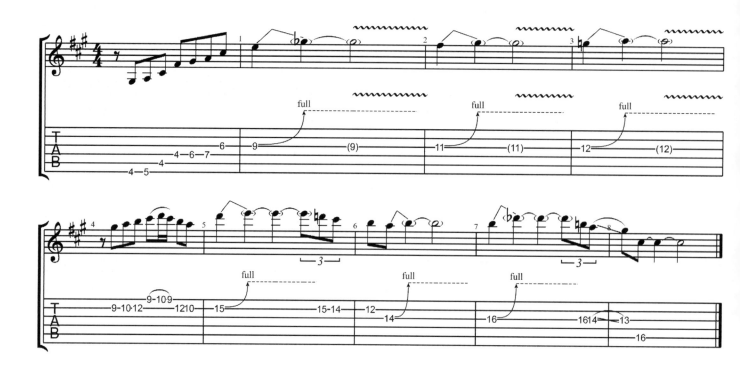

As the solo begins to develop there is a change in the use of rhythmic subdivisions. In Example 2k, you can see just from the shape of the line that I contrast fast runs with more vocal-like string bending phrases.

Bar one has a rapid picked 1/16th note scale run that transitions into the first string bend in bar two. I also change my melodic approach here by adding chromatic passing notes into the A Major/F# Minor scale pattern.

As mentioned in Chapter One, in jazz, where soloists typically use lots of passing notes, the aim is to play chord/scale tones mostly on the strong beats of the bar and passing notes mostly on the weaker beats. This is a way of *grounding* a line, so that the listener can keep in touch with the harmony. It's not a hard and fast rule, but if you're new to experimenting with chromatic notes, starting this way will help you develop your technique. I always aim for a strong chord tone to conclude a line (as in bar four).

Example 2k

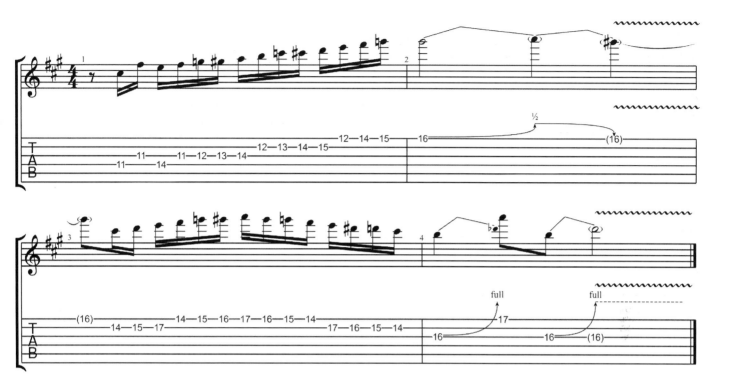

Example 2l picks up from the previous line and again mixes up the rhythmic phrasing. The line begins with an ascending 1/8th note run that targets the E note on the second string, 17th fret, and bends it up a full tone.

Bars 3-4 then move into a rapid-picked 1/16th note run. As you can see, there are a lot of chromatic notes in this phrase and they make the line sound more complex than you might think.

The line is based around this very basic F# Minor Pentatonic box shape:

F# Minor Pentatonic

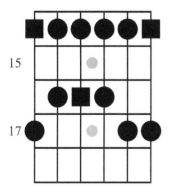

F# Minor Pentatonic has the notes F#, A, B, C# and E. If we analyze the lick, we see that it begins on an A note (a scale tone played on a strong beat), then uses chromatic notes to target the next scale tone (F#) that fits into the box shape.

The next part of the phrase uses passing notes to target the E note on the second string in the box shape. After this, I apply some variation to the idea to stop it sounding too predictable, but the whole time I'm visualizing that pentatonic shape and working within it.

The whole lick ends on the F# scale tone, which is also played on a strong beat. Remember that the line should be played with strict down-up alternate picking.

You can experiment with this idea yourself by taking a box position shape and composing licks that include passing notes. A good way to start is by picking specific scale tone target notes and using passing notes to approach them.

Example 21

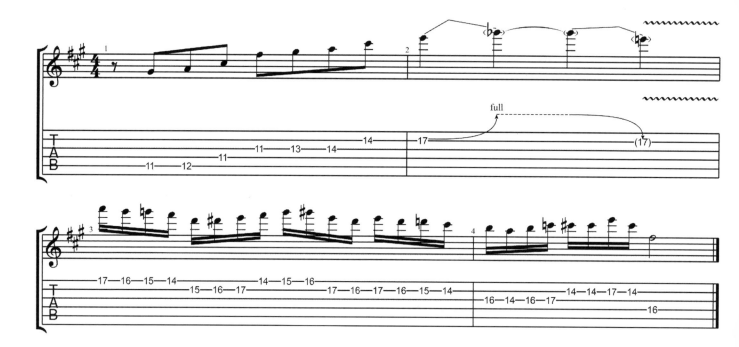

After the 1/16th note passages of the last two examples, the tune ends with some strongly accented ascending power chords.

This section is made up of two guitar parts working in conjunction. First, here is the main rhythm part. The chords move up in whole steps: D5 – E5 – F#5 and are played as two accented 1/8th notes on the first beat of each bar. Nothing is played in bars four and eight. It's a simple, perhaps clichéd rhythm part, but it leaves plenty of space to counterpoint it with another guitar.

Example 2m

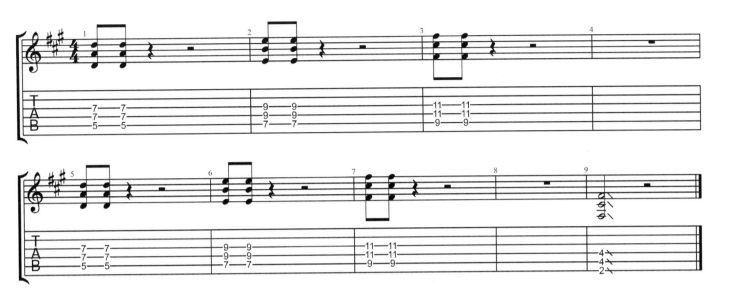

To complement the previous part, the other guitar plays in the rhythmic space that is left. First, the chords are outlined, landing on beat 3 of bars 1-3. Here I'm using either 4th intervals (bar one) or triads (bars two-three). When you play this, apply some fretting hand vibrato for extra sustain and texture.

Then, in bar four, a change in rhythm with a phrase played in octaves signals the start of a new idea. In bars 5-8 the second guitar part plays in unison with the first, and also adds fills with double-stops.

To end the solo, I return to single-notes and some string bends to end the phrase clearly on the home chord of F# minor.

Example 2n

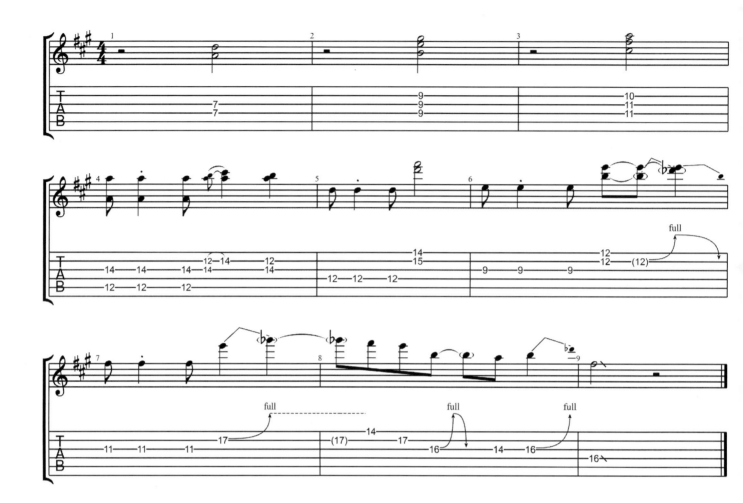

Full Solo

Example 2o is the recorded guitar solo in its entirety and it's worth taking a moment to think about how you'll approach playing it. You've already practiced the components individually, but these licks will sound and work slightly differently in the context of the whole.

Begin by listening to the whole solo a couple of times before attempting it, so you have an *aural map* of the territory you're going to cover.

The first eight bars don't present too many technical difficulties, but there are more challenging sections to play at tempo from bar nine onwards. It might be worth spending some time playing 1/16th notes to a metronome to begin with. The backing track for this tune is 160bpm but start slower and gradually work your way up to full tempo.

To improve speed and picking accuracy, I advocate the following approach:

- Spend a few minutes just warming up

- Pick any scale pattern and play up and down it at a comfortable tempo that produces near-perfect results

- Take a short rest, then increase the tempo by a small amount (between 5 and 10bpm) and repeat

- Increase the tempo every few minutes until mistakes become unavoidable

- Go a bit quicker still, and don't worry about the inevitable mistakes

- Now, return to the fastest tempo at which you can play completely error-free

If you persist with this exercise for, say, 20 minutes of a practice session, you'll find that the speed at which you can play without making a mistake has increased. In the long run, the only way to increase your speed and accuracy is to be forced to play at tempos that are slightly beyond you. The more you play on the edge, the more your playing will improve at slower tempos.

Returning to the solo, isolate any parts that you're having difficulty with and drill these at a slower tempo to build muscle memory. Once the fretting hand movements are committed to muscle memory, you're free to focus on picking hand efficiency.

Once you have each section of the solo under your fingers, you can work on the nuances, such as vibrato and how dynamics are applied to each phrase. A good final goal would be to play along note for note with the original recording. Then, of course, you can jam along to the backing track and work on your own ideas.

Example 2o

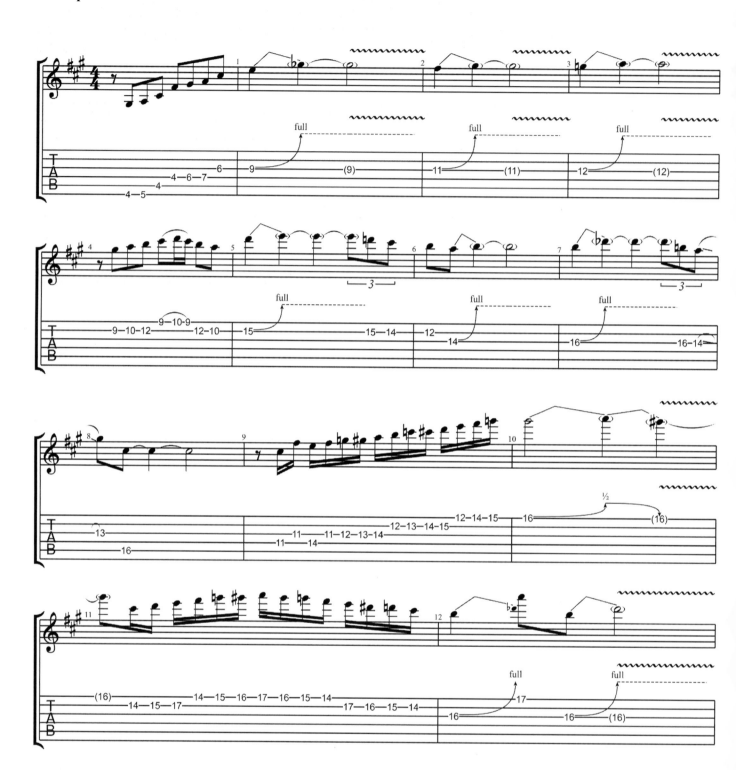

Chapter Three – Minor-Focus Melodic Phrasing

About the track

In this chapter we're going to explore some minor blues vocabulary over a mid-tempo hard rock track. The idea behind this track is a blues with a twist. Although it has the sound/feel of a blues, along with some of the chords you'd expect to see in a standard blues sequence, it actually has an AABA format and is organized into eight-bar sections.

First of all, let's break down the rhythm parts, so you can see what's happening in each section.

This track begins with a classic hard rock rhythm guitar part based around an E5 chord played in the open position. The riff is syncopated using 1/8th and 1/16th notes and also includes some quarter tone bends on the low E string. Notice how the 1/16th note punctuations on beat 4 of each bar jump out in the mix while the other parts are resting. This is a great way to get rhythm guitar parts to interlock effectively.

Example 3a

Example 3b illustrates the second half of the A Section where the harmony briefly moves up a minor 3rd to G5.

Here, there is a busier rhythm part that moves from intervals of a 5th to a major 6th (bar one) followed by a short bluesy 1/16th note figure. The G chord has replaced the IV chord (A) in the harmony, but it lasts for the expected two bars before returning to the E5 riff of the previous example.

Example 3b

The whole A section repeats and is followed by the B Section below. The chords of this section sound like the turnaround part of a blues but are repeated to form another eight-bar section.

The rhythm part begins with the V chord, a second inversion B5 (or B/F#) and moves to the IV chord (A5) before repeating the E5 riff. In bar three, the root of the B chord is played and a D5/A replaces the straight IV chord.

The whole thing repeats before ending with steady 1/8th note palm-muted chugs on the D5 chord in bar eight.

Example 3c

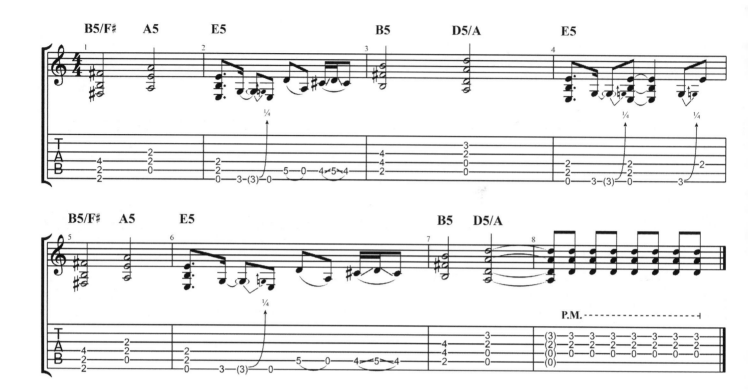

You'll hear the A and B sections repeat throughout the tune. Now let's look at the melodic ideas I came up with to play over the backing.

For the melody over the A section, in bars 1-4 I play short call and response phrases primarily using 1/16th notes punctuated with 1/4 note bends. When playing these lines, you can dig in quite hard and apply plenty of vibrato to the last note in each bar.

In bar three I add a pinched harmonic to the last D note. Pinch harmonics are achieved by picking downward then immediately muting the picked string lightly with the flesh of the thumb that sits behind the pick.

This line is all about the embellishment and shows how a simple melody can be enhanced by articulations like bent notes, vibrato and harmonics.

Example 3d

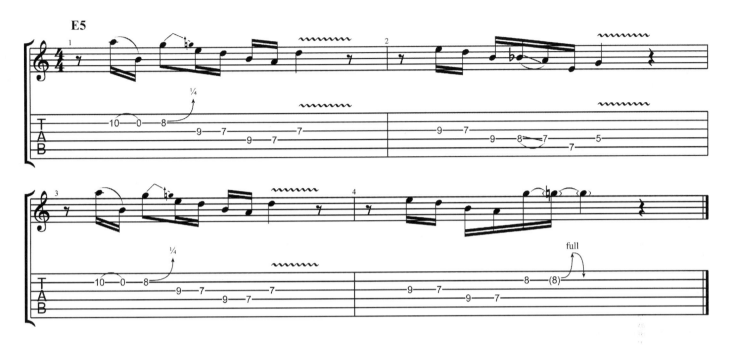

Example 3e is the melody I came up with for the second half of the A section. The notes come from the G Mixolydian scale (G A B C D E F) and the main idea is to emphasize 6th intervals, although there is a mixture of 4ths, 5ths and 6ths.

The rhythm is syncopated using a combination of 1/16th and tied 1/8th notes and the melody begins on the "1&" of bar one so that the phrase crosses the bar line into the second bar.

Example 3e

Next comes the repeat of the A Section and it's time to introduce a new melodic idea.

The melody in Example 3f begins with longer note durations and sustained string bending with lots of vibrato. Make the most of the articulation here. The ability to bend notes is one of the key weapons in our arsenal as guitar players and you should inject these bends with all the emotion you can muster.

Be sure to bend the full tone before adding vibrato. Vibrato style is a personal choice and many players can be identified by how they apply this embellishment alone (think of Angus Young, for instance, who has a very distinctive fast approach). Think about the sound that appeals to you, whether it's rapid vibrato, Angus-style, or slow and wide.

In bar three, more rhythmic interest is created with 1/16th note groupings and a descending run using the E Mixolydian scale (E F# G# A B C# D) with a couple of chromatic passing notes that help to keep the phrase flowing.

Example 3f

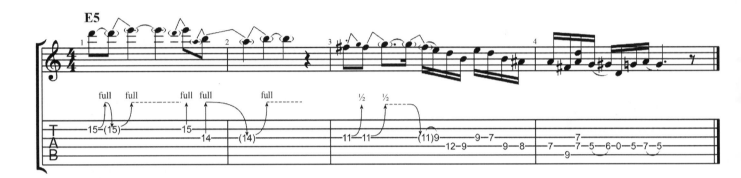

For the second half of the A section the lick begins with a fourth string bend to the major 3rd of the G chord and the line uses the G Mixolydian scale. This transitions into an E Minor Pentatonic lick in bars 3-4. Listen out for the embellishments to the line, with some rapid vibrato and pinch harmonics.

Example 3g

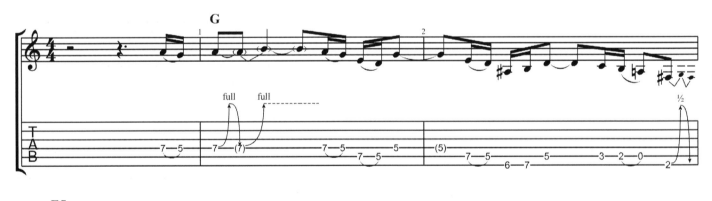

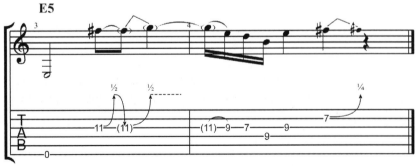

Now we come to the turnaround section that has been expanded into an eight-bar format.

Over the B5/F# in bar one, the whole step bends simply target the root of the chord. Then, to transition from the A5 to E5 chord, more bends take us into the familiar 12th position E Minor Pentatonic box shape.

After the bend at the beginning of bar two, there is a chromatic run down. Notice that I'm hitting E Minor Pentatonic scale tones on the strong beats of the bar, which helps to keep the lick rooted in the harmony, even though there are a lot of passing notes.

The chromatic run leads into the phrase that begins bar three. This time, to outline the B5 and A5 chords, I'm just using the E Natural Minor scale (E F# G A B C D). The lick here has its roots in country rock.

Example 3h

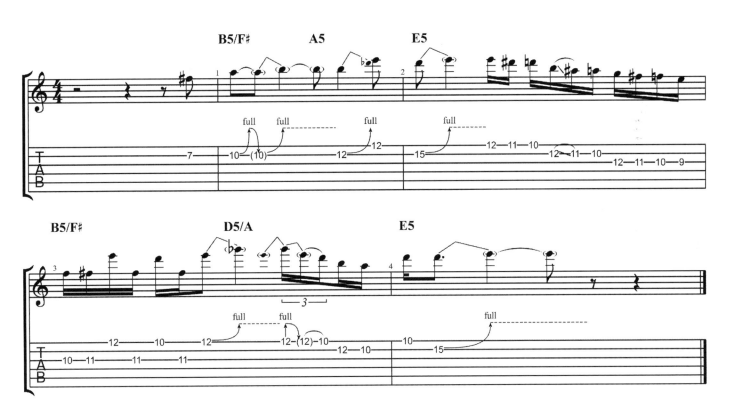

As the turnaround repeats, I play a busier melodic line with predominantly 1/16th note phrasing. You'll notice that much of this line uses the top three strings only. Often, it's great to use a wide range of the neck, but depending on what is happening with the other instrumentation sometimes it's better to restrict your lines to a smaller range, so that they fit "in the mix".

The note choices here are very much dictated by the underlying chord changes, rather than just blowing with the parent scale, and the important chord tones are emphasized.

In bar one, notice that I quote the short lick that appeared in bar three of the previous example, over B5/F#. It quickly moves into a different idea, but repeating and adapting short motifs like this helps to give our solos a sense of continuity.

At the end of bar one, you may recognize the last three notes as a D major triad, though the chord at this point in the progression is A5. Superimposed over an A bass note, a D major triad creates the sound of A6sus.

In bar two, the E Natural Minor scale-based descending run is punctuated with bends to make the line more interesting and help it to float over the groove. The run down is targeting the F# note that falls on beat 1 of bar three, which is the major 3rd of the B chord.

The three-note ascending phrase spells a B5 chord, while the descending three-note phrase implies B minor, in anticipation of the D chord that is coming. When the D chord lands, I play a D major triad before heading into the string bending section of the final bar.

Example 3i

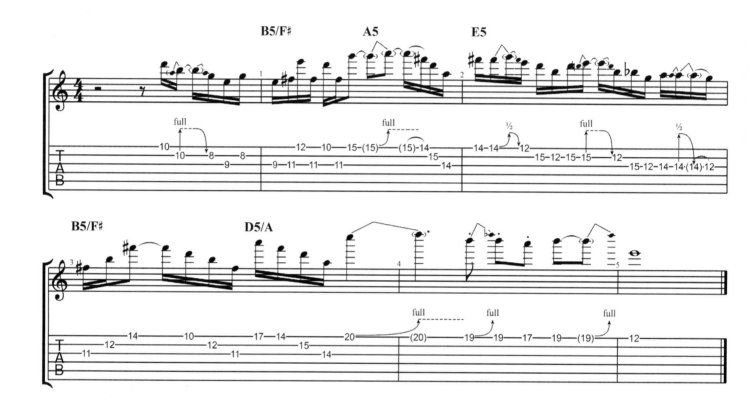

The next section of the tune is the repeat of the A Section. At this point, I felt it was time to introduce a completely new idea and, thinking compositionally, opted for a three-part harmony passage. The resulting parts create a mood-shift in the music and the idea I had was to create harmony parts that cascaded downwards.

Example 3j shows the first part, composed almost entirely of 1/16th notes and beginning around 8th position on the fretboard, gradually descending to 5th position. You'll hear that the overall theme of the line takes a call and response approach. Bars 1-2 are the call statement and bars 3-4 make the response, then the whole thing repeats.

In bars 5-8, although I play identical melodic line, the underlying harmony has shifted a minor third from E to G, so the notes take on a different intervallic flavor.

Example 3j (audio for examples 3j, 3k, 3l combined)

The second harmony part echoes the first rhythmically, using a stream of 1/16th notes but is harmonized diatonically with the first part using notes from the E Natural Minor scale. The part uses lots of 4th and 5th intervals to create the harmony.

If you're going to overlay a harmony guitar part like this, then it demands some attention to detail. It's obviously important that one part tracks the other as tightly as possible, but accuracy when bending notes is particularly important, so that there is no blurring of the harmony.

Example 3k

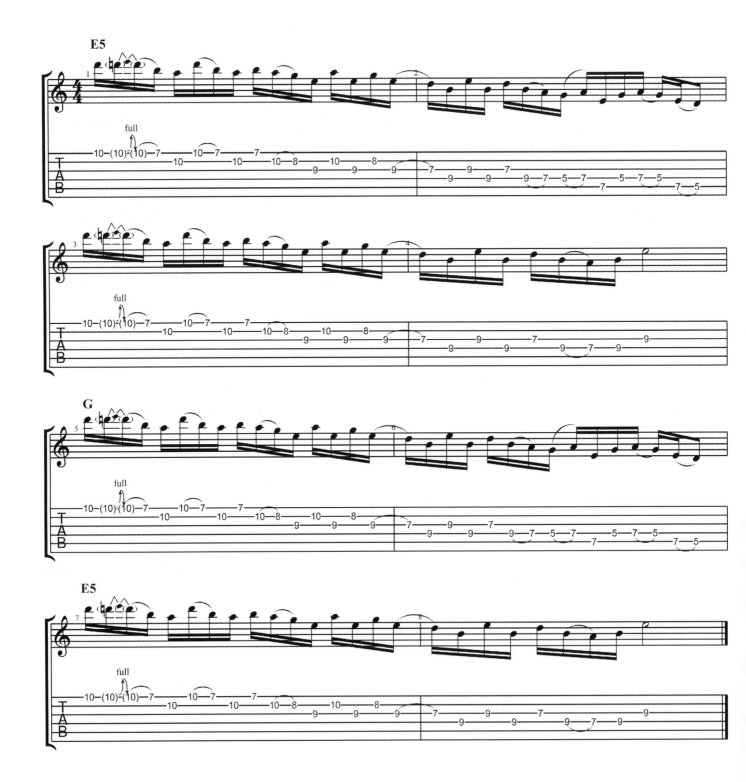

The third guitar part is designed to soar over the top of the other two, with long sustained notes, and almost takes on the role of a synth part. Key chord tones are spelt out, beginning with the E root note in bar one and the 5th of the G chord in bar five. I also play the 5th against the final E5 chord. I'm using both whole-step and half step bends in this part to help the melody sound like a string player might play it.

Example 31

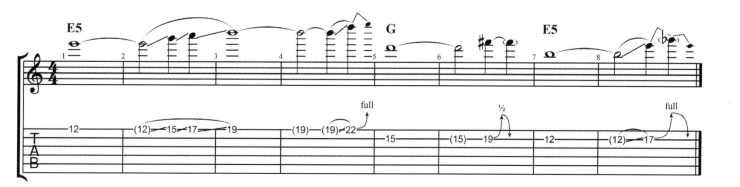

Next comes the B Section again.

This time around, the B Section is used like a middle eight for the tune and the backing breaks down to drums and bass only. Throughout this section, two guitars interact, sometimes hitting harmony notes. The high guitar plays the part shown in the previous example, while the new guitar focuses on fast runs that terminate in bends, hitting target notes.

In bar one, we kick off with two whole step bends that cross into bar two. Then, two fast sextuplet runs are launched from beats 3 and 4. You may be inclined to play this type of run legato, but you know that my style is to alternate pick everything, and I prefer the attack and clarity of this approach.

It makes sense to organize triplet-based lines like this into a three-note-per-string configuration, which opens up the possibility of using economy alternate picking. i.e. begin with a downstroke and pick down-up-down for the three notes on the D string. The final downward pick motion then transitions onto the adjacent G string to begin the next three-note grouping with a downward pick, and so on.

The idea of an ascending run transitioning into a bend repeats in bars 4-5, and this section ends with a composed melodic lick with more bends.

Example 3m

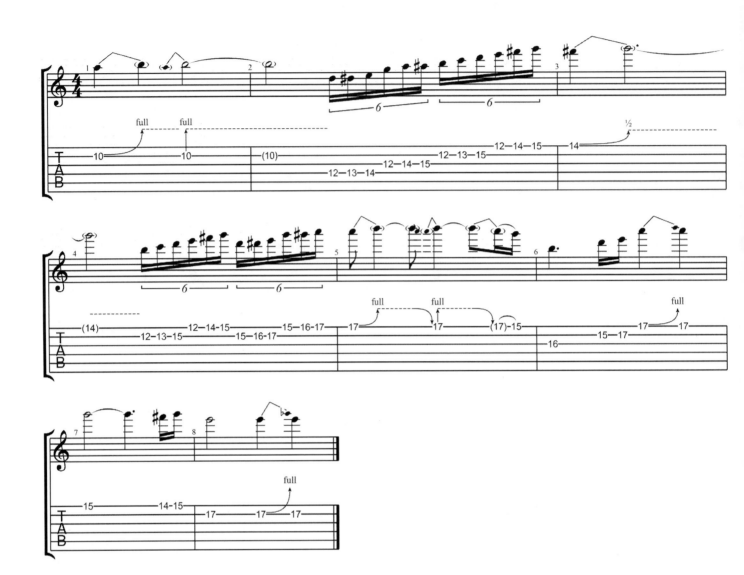

Now we come to the main solo over the tune that spans thirty-two bars. We're going break it down into smaller sections to look at the ideas being used, then at the end of the chapter you can play through the whole thing.

The opening statement below uses a succession of 1/4 note bends and is based around the E Blues scale. This morphs into an E Mixolydian line in bar three and the first half of bar four. Then, as a way of setting up the melodic idea that will follow in Example 3o, I play an intervallic passage on the top strings that includes a string skip. Notice that the top line of the interval lick is descending chromatically on the first string.

Example 3n

Example 3o is a motif lick based around the 12th position pentatonic box shape and uses repeating whole step bends. It's a southern rock kind of idea and uses wide vibrato for effect.

Example 3o

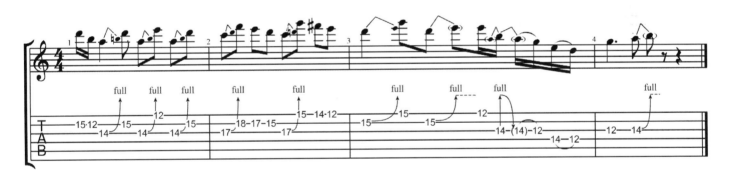

Example 3p continues the country rock theme and bar two features some 1/8th note bends using a pedal tone idea. Some are deliberately played on the offbeat for rhythmic variety. Bars 4-5 move to a country-inspired single-note 1/16th run. Notice here that to keep things from becoming too linear, I change direction and skip strings throughout.

Example 3p

To create some contrast with the previous part, Example 3q is based in the lower register, but the string-bending articulations are continued. Check out the audio to catch the attack and dynamics used here.

Example 3q

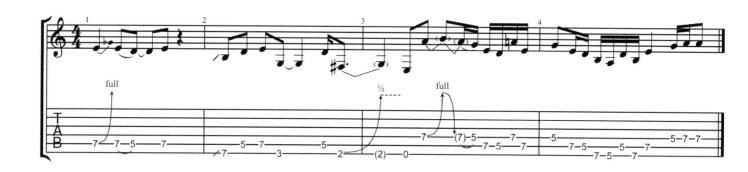

At the chord change in bar one of the next example, I rapidly change register and move back into 12th position for some bends with longer note durations. It's not necessary to play fast runs all the time; soul and expression are nearly always more effective in engaging an audience.

Bar four features another intervallic passage played on non-adjacent strings. This time, I'm using a pedal tone with an E note on the fourth string, fret 14, while descending chromatically above on the second string.

Example 3r

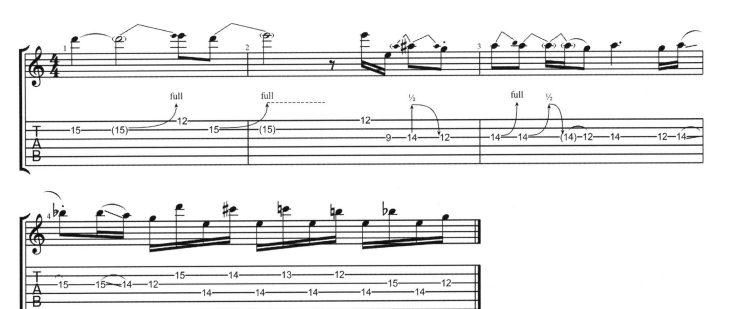

The next example demonstrates how you can easily mix rhythms to great effect even within a few bars. Here I begin with two whole step bends but quickly play a sextuplet run to take me up to the high string bend at the beginning of bar two. For the next two bars I'm playing longer note durations with more string bends before a 1/16th note descending run in the final bar.

Let's take a closer look at that final run, which is played over the D5 chord that turns the tune around. It's based around the D Major scale and uses chromatic passing notes to target the scale tones (notice the D major triad that falls on the "2&" of the bar). You'll hear that this a repeating motif.

Example 3s

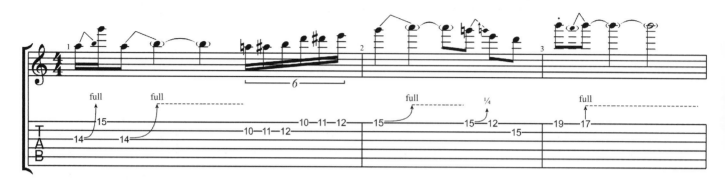

In bars 25-28 of the solo, shown in Example 3t below, I'm playing a pre-composed 1/16th note pattern that is building toward the end of the track. Spanning all four middle strings, this motif is built around an E minor triad voiced over an interval of a 10th.

One thing I really like about the approach of alternate picking is how it's possible to make un-guitaristic parts come alive. When you're playing through a distorted amp with lots of sustain, often just playing one note can work really well – but using good alternate picking we can also play more complex passages in a one-note-at-a-time fashion. Alternate picking can produce the note clarity we need to play intervallic passages, but also runs that would sound less clear played legato, unless you're extremely good at it.

To practice this idea, crank up your amp and turn on the distortion, then play some arpeggio passages. Don't allow the notes to bleed into one another, but with alternate picking and some picking hand damping, aim to sound each note as clearly and cleanly as possible. Once you're playing with great note separation, then begin to increase the tempo and work at maintaining the clarity.

Example 3t

The motif introduced in the last example is now modified to a G Major tonality for the first two bars of Example 3u before returning to E Major at the track's conclusion.

Rhythmically this is a little different from previous example and includes some offbeat 1/16th notes. Watch out for your picking accuracy on the string skips as before.

Example 3u

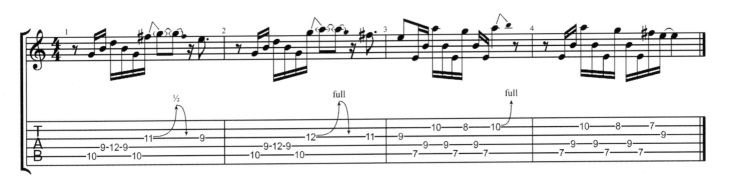

Full Solo

Now it's time to tackle the full solo. You already know to isolate any difficult parts and practice them more slowly, so instead I want to suggest some practice ideas to work on that will help you play some of the more challenging sections.

For sections like bars five and twenty, where you are playing intervals, make up some etudes of your own that use similar intervals or include pedal tones. I love Classical music and composers like J.S. Bach often used melodic motifs in their music that are similar to the ideas here.

To get to grips with the rapid 1/16th note triplets that I often use when soloing, work on your three-note-per-string patterns. As I've done in this solo, you can add chromatic notes into scale patterns to spice up the lines. Add passing notes to diatonic scale patterns you are already familiar with to create long, flowing lines.

As a final thought, listen carefully to how I use devices like string bending, vibrato and pinch harmonics. Try playing a lick you know well, but embellish it in several different ways to see how much variety you can squeeze out of it. Working on these techniques will instantly make you a more musical-sounding player.

Enjoy learning the solo and make your final goal to be able to play along with the recording.

Example 3v

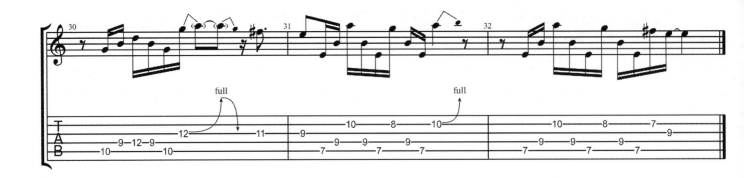

Chapter Four – Creating Tension and Resolution

So far, we've explored melodic soloing vocabulary over dominant 7, major, and minor tonalities. In this chapter, we're going to bring together some of the phrasing ideas we've learned and apply them over a hard rock blues.

As you're probably aware, it's very common in the blues for soloists to switch between minor and major pentatonic ideas, and to do so over chords that are frequently played as dominant 7s. This "blurring" of the harmony in the blues allows us to work with a broader melodic palette, and draw from many different tonalities to play lines.

Additionally, the solid, predictable blues progression is the ideal canvas on which to play more "outside" sounding lines, since the listener is already familiar with the predictable basic harmony.

Here, I've played four successive short solos over a blues in D, each taking a slightly different approach. I've used chromatic passing notes in order to spice up the lines and keep things interesting and, in the final solo, I played some outside-inside passages that challenge the harmony even more.

First, a quick run-down of what's happening with the rhythm guitar part in the backing. The backing track comes with your free audio download, so you can practice the solos and jam along with it later.

The Rhythm Part

The rhythm guitar is tuned to Drop D (the low E string is tuned down a whole step to D, leaving the rest of the strings tuned normally), which adds some harmonic resonance and depth to the sound. The rhythm part uses various power chord forms to create the riff accompaniment (either root plus 5th, or root, 5th and octave/9th). Subtle rhythmic variations create contrast within the part.

Example 4a shows the four-bar turnaround section of the tune, which is used as an introduction to the first solo.

Beginning in bar one with a sustained A5 power chord, a half step bend is added on beat three to give the part some air before another power chord (G5add9) is played on the downbeat of bar two.

Bars 3-7 switch gears rhythmically to 1/16th notes combined with off beat 1/8th notes, to make the part distinctive, rather than relying on sustained power chords throughout. Note the use of palm muting in bar three.

Example 4a

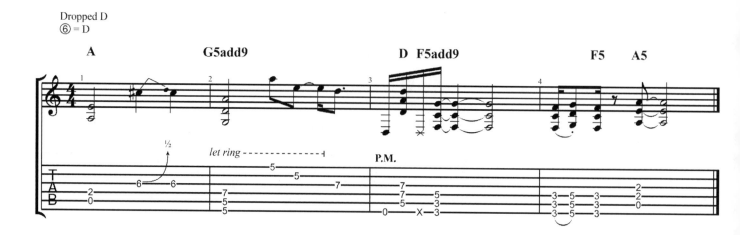

Example 4b shows the first four bars of the blues progression. 1/16th and 1/8th note rhythms are combined to form a syncopated riff. The low open D string is used throughout, so use palm muting to dynamically punctuate the lower register notes. This will also help to provide separation in the mix and keep the part sounding clear.

Simple rhythmic devices help to give the riff a groove, based around two-bar phrases. Bars one and three both have a rest on the final 1/4 note beat to create space, while bars two and four both feature a 1/16th note *push* on the final power chord which anticipates the beat.

Example 4b

As we move to the IV chord (G5), the rhythm part again mixes 1/16th and 1/8th note rhythms. In bar one, the G5 chord is moved down a half step to F5 to make the harmony more interesting. In bar two, the rhythmic focus is off beat 1/16th notes, with ghosted notes and palm muting.

Bars 3-4 return to the D-based riff of the previous example, and bars 5-8 repeat the turnaround tag seen in Example 4a.

Throughout, the open low D string glues the part together.

Example 4c

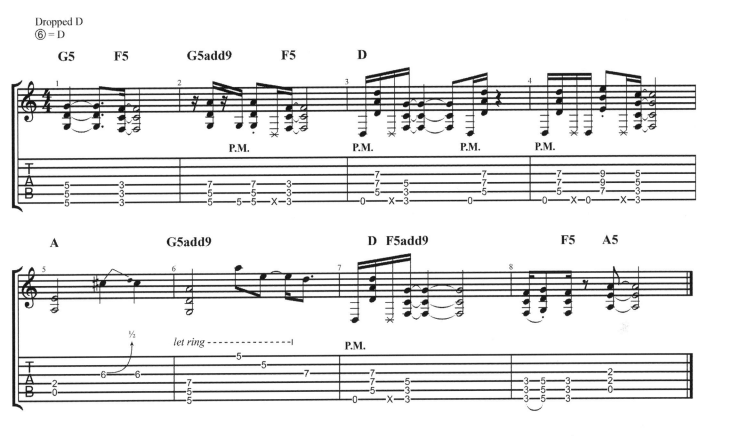

Now we've worked through the rhythm part, we turn our attention to soloing over this tune.

As always, our aim should be to think *compositionally* when constructing our solos. We can use the phrasing devices demonstrated in previous chapters to build melodic lines (motifs, question and answer phrasing, etc.), so that the solo has a strong structure and something to say.

On the audio, you'll hear that I play *four* separate solos, following on from one another. I change my tone slightly for each one, so you can clearly hear where one solo ends and the next one begins.

Now, I'll break down each solo for you and explain the ideas in use. After you've worked your way through all of the section examples, you can have a go at the complete solo, connecting them all together.

Solo 1 begins with a riff-like idea that establishes a theme for the solo. The phrases begin on the off beat (apart from bar three) and use 1/16th note rhythms. Repeating the same rhythm throughout helps to glue the idea together. I also played this with a heavy swing feel to create a groove. Although the line is played with a heavy rock tone, it could be seen as a country guitar idea (always an influence in my playing) with its use of open strings throughout.

There are also some half step approach notes here to make the harmony a little more colorful. They add movement between the minor and major 3rd of the chord in bar one, and the 5th and b5 (blues scale) in bars 1-2.

Example 4d

We've learned throughout this book that we can take a thematic idea then develop it, and that's where we're going next. The next section of the solo continues the 1/16th note rhythmic idea and continues to incorporate open strings. Here, the open strings are used to launch the finger slides played on adjacent strings.

Since this part of the tune is focused on the IV chord (G) of the blues progression, the open G string is played throughout and acts as a drone note, interspersed with scale steps.

We're also emphasizing chord tones in this line (such as the major 3rd and 5th in the first two beats of bar one), so that listeners can immediately relate to the idea.

Example 4e

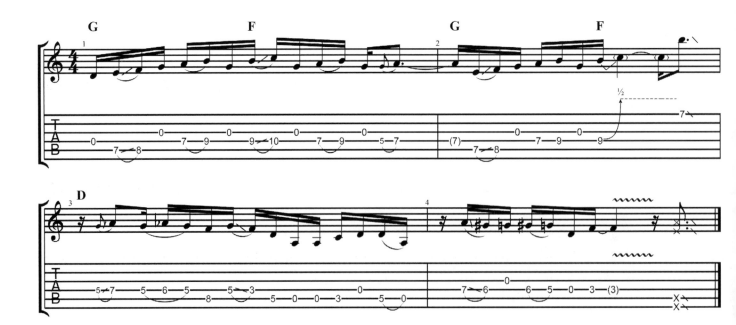

Example 4f continues to build on the ideas that began the solo. Here we retain some of the phrasing concepts (beginning each phrase on the off beat, using mainly 1/16th notes, and incorporating open strings) while introducing a new idea. In this part of the solo, string bends are used to make the phrasing float over the beat.

When we think of string bending, it's often the high notes that spring to mind, but bending in the lower register can be highly effective and that's the approach I've taken here.

Listen to how I play it on the audio, then aim for precision and accuracy with your bends. Always visualize and hear the note you're aiming for when launching a bend, rather than just bending and hoping for the best.

Example 4f

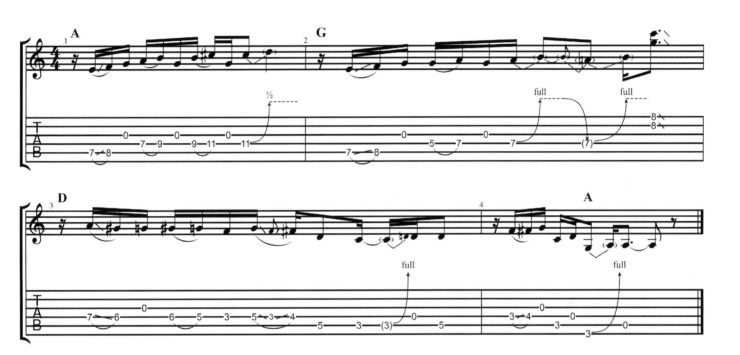

The next example is the start of Solo 2. Here we wipe the slate clean and start over, to explore some different ideas.

One simple thing you can do that will benefit any solo is to use contrasting rhythms. This line begins with a whole step bend that targets the 5th (A) of the D chord. From this starting part, the rhythmic intensity of the line is allowed to build over subsequent bars.

It is a simple idea, but techniques like starting slow and getting faster, starting quietly and getting louder, or playing low and transitioning to playing high just work, so we shouldn't dismiss their simplicity.

This line also features more half step approach notes, especially in bar three. I'm often emphasizing the 3rd of the D chord, sometimes via a string bend and sometimes via a hammer-on, and also the 5th/b5 tonality of the blues scale.

At the end of this line, the repeated bends are used to help us transition to the IV chord and on the audio, you'll hear the final bend carry over into bar one of Example 4h.

Example 4g

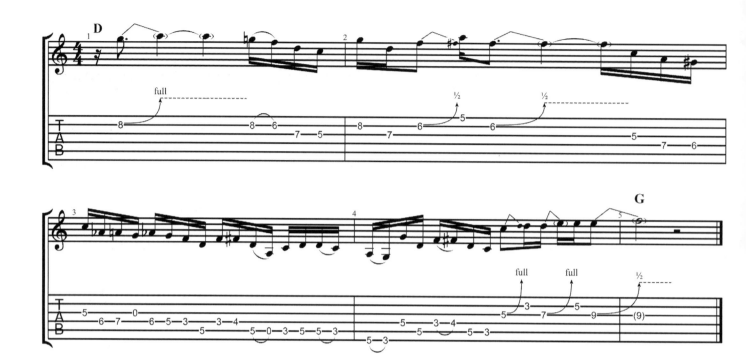

The series of bends that ended the previous idea help to ramp up the intensity of the solo and pave the way for playing more complex ideas. To transition from the IV chord bars back to the I, we have a line composed from evenly spaced 1/16th notes. Again, played clean and in a different context, this could be considered a country guitar lick, where half step approach notes are used to target important chord tones of the underlying harmony.

In bars 3-4, I move away from this idea and play a series of double-stops which bring a different kind of rhythmic punctuation to the solo. The first double-stop phrase uses a chromatic descent from the 10th fret to the 7th to land on the root and 3rd of a D major chord.

This phrase is repeated immediately, so that it crosses the bar line, but is shifted up a minor third to descend from the 13th fret to the 10th. This time the notes are F and A, which are the b3 and 5th of a D minor chord.

The line ends with a series of high register string bends, with the final bend held over the bar line to segue into the next example.

Example 4h

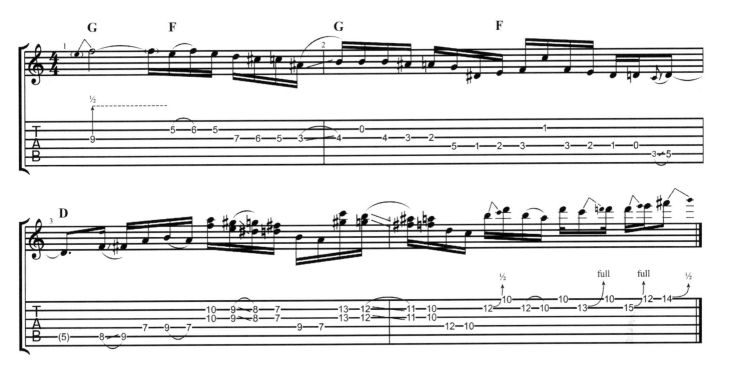

The first two bars of the next idea use a long 1/16th note line that includes a lot of chromatic approach notes. The idea in play here is to target chord tones, approaching them from four frets above or below. In bar one, the first target is the E note on the first string, 12th fret, approached chromatically from above (E is the 5th of A major). The E note is targeted a second time in this bar.

Beginning at the end of bar one and transitioning into bar two, the next target is the B note that falls on the 1& of bar two, and is approached chromatically from below (B is the 3rd of the underlying G major chord).

Using multiple chromatic approach notes is a technique employed by many jazz guitar players. As long as you are hitting chord tones mostly on the strong beats of the bar, the listener can tolerate a lot of notes from outside the key and will still get a clear sense of the harmony. This is a great way to add some tension to your solo lines and break away from purely diatonic licks.

Be sure not to rush the 1/16th notes. It's easy to think, "Now I have to play faster" and push ahead of the beat, but you have more time than you think.

Example 4i

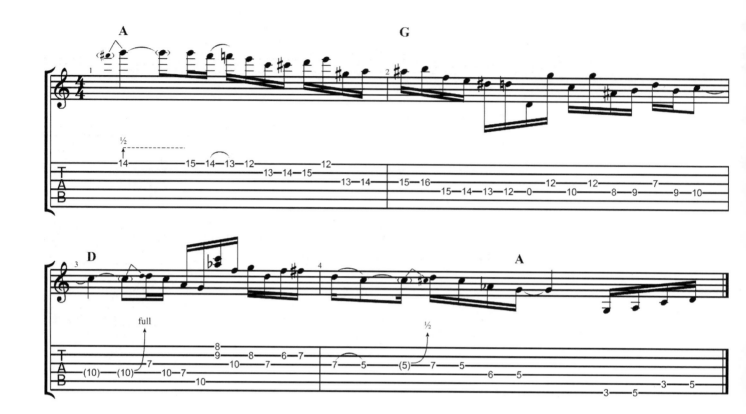

Next, we're onto the third solo, and we begin with a motif-driven line that uses repetitive phrasing to tell the story. When you put all of these ideas together at the end of this chapter, you'll notice that the amount of chromatic notes being used increases from solo to solo.

The blues, with its simple harmony and three basic chords, is the ideal vehicle to road-test some outside-inside playing and the final solo will push the boundaries of this approach.

Every solo should begin with a strong opening statement, and here is a two-bar phrase that uses a repeating bend idea.

This is followed in bars 3-4 with what I'd describe as a chromatic motif. These 1/16th note phrases are displaced to avoid playing similar phrases in the same place in the bar each time. Notice that each time the phrase repeats, its top note is ascending the high E string.

An idea like this helps to add some drama to the solo and creates the sense that it is heading towards a destination or climax.

Example 4j

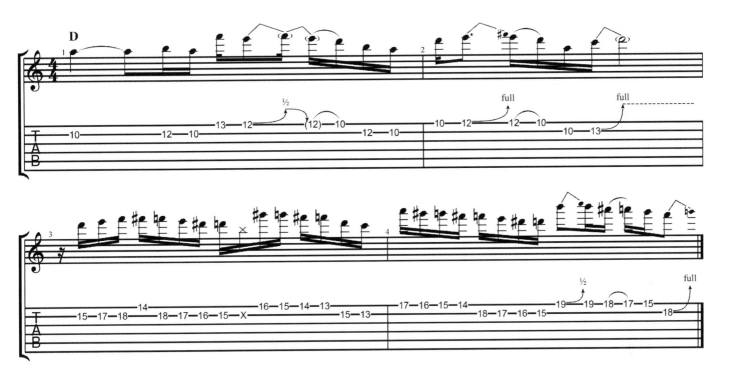

Next, we move to the IV chord and mix up the rhythms to create some variety in the phrasing. After playing phrases with more space in bars 1-2, bar three begins a chromatic 1/16th note lick.

Bar three features a similar use of passing notes, but here the thinking is scalic. I'm playing around with the D Blues scale (D F G Ab A C) but filling out groups of four notes with chromatic passing notes.

In the first group of four notes, for example, the note C is in the scale but the B that follows is not. The next note (A#) is also a non-scale tone, but the A that follows is. The next four-note group features three scale tones and one passing note, and so on.

Introducing outside notes as part of a rhythmically strong phrase makes it easier for listeners to accept the momentary dissonance and it's a very useful way of creating tension and resolution in the music.

Example 4k

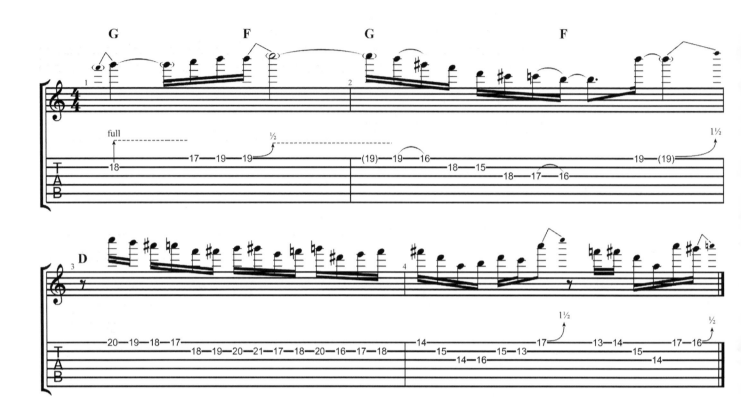

For the last part of Solo 3, we begin by allowing the lead guitar to mirror the rhythm guitar part. Listening and reacting to what's happening around you when soloing is a great skill to develop and brings cohesion to any band setting. In bar one, the solo line plays the riff note for note in the high register, and in bar two this idea is echoed to make bars 1-2 a question and answer phrase.

There is a mixture of half step and one-and-a-half-step bends in this line, so listen carefully to what is being played and focus on achieving good pitch accuracy.

Example 41

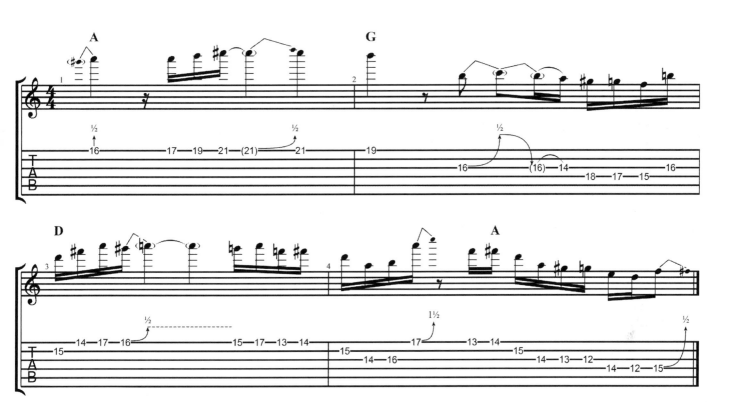

Finally, Solo 4. The focus of this tune has been to spice up a potentially routine blues solo and add much more movement and interest. To round things off, here's a solo that features more outside soloing ideas.

This solo cuts straight to the outside tensions and you may wonder what's going on in bars 1-2 with the angular sounding line, so let's break it down and analyze the musical ideas at work.

Bar one uses the Half-Whole Diminished scale (D, Eb, F, F#, Ab, A, B, C) to produce a rich set of tension notes over the D7 chord. If we analyze the notes of the scale and compare them to the notes of D7 (D, F#, A, C), we get a combination of chord tones, extended, and altered tones. In order, they are:

D = root note of D7

Eb = b9 (though the Eb note is not used in this lick)

F = #9

F# = 3rd

Ab/G# = #11

A = 5th

B = 13th

C = 7th

The Half-Whole scale (so called because it follows a repeating pattern of half and whole steps on the fretboard) played from the root note of a dominant chord is a great choice for outside-inside playing, because it contains every chord tone, the extended 13th note, then a collection of altered tones.

Playing D Half-Whole over D7 we can, for example, instantly create the sound of a D13 chord, or D#9, or Db5#9 etc. If you've not experimented with this scale before, below is a useful pattern for playing it that crawls up the neck. Robben Ford has made great use of this scale in his playing over the years.

D Half-Whole Scale Pattern

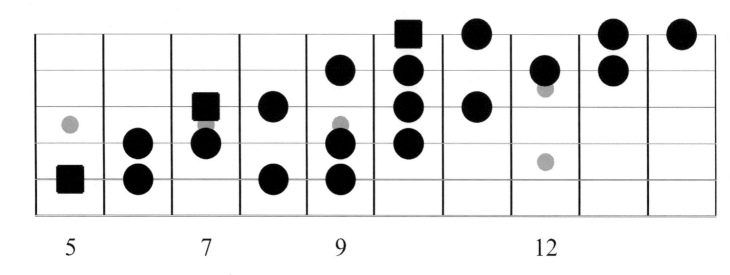

The line continues with D Half-Whole Diminished into the first half of bar two, then I switch scale for a different sound.

In the second half of bar two, I transition into the D Harmonic Minor scale (D, E, F, G, A, Bb/A#, C#). This creates an equally tense but different sound. Over the D7 harmony, the notes unique to D Harmonic Minor create the following colors:

E = 9th

G = 11th

Bb/A# = #5 or b13

Combining these two scales to create one long line means that we have all the chord tones and every possible altered tension. For reference, here's a useful scale pattern for D Harmonic Minor.

D Harmonic Minor scale pattern

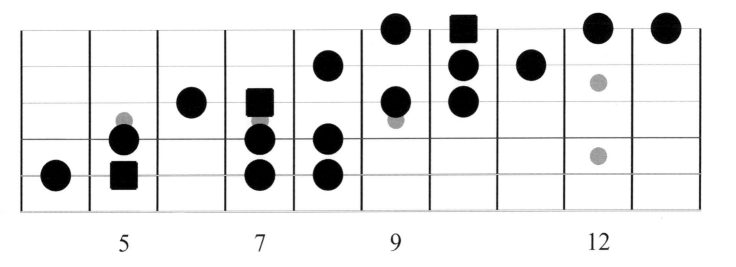

After the sustained bent notes, we return to the D Half-Whole Diminished scale in bars 3-4 to close out the lick.

Example 4m

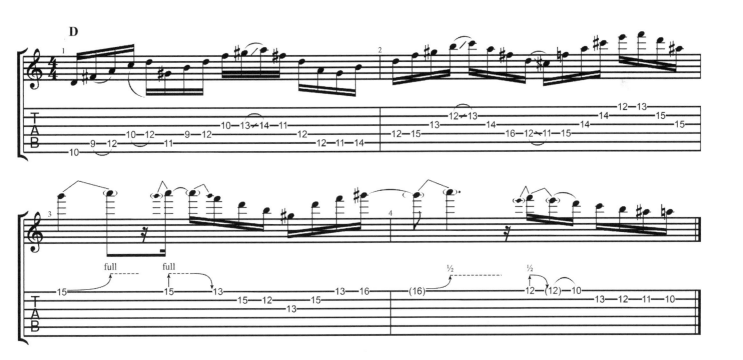

In the next section of the tune, we know that the harmony alternates between G and F chords before returning to the tonic. G is the blues IV chord, but the passing F chord is played for the same duration and given equal weight. We can make either chord the focal point of our melodic ideas.

In bar one, I'm thinking of the F chord as the main tonal center and use a substitution idea to construct the melodic line. Jazz musicians often use a device called *implied harmony*. In simple layman's terms, it's pretending that a chord belongs to a different tonality or serves a different function in a piece of music.

Here, I'm viewing the F chord as a IV chord in its own right. That means it could resolve to either C Major or C Minor as its implied parent key. The minor tonality fits best with the mood of the music, so I'm using the C Harmonic Minor scale, implying that at this point in the music we've changed key to C Minor. Superimposing the notes of C Harmonic Minor (C, D, Eb, F, G, Ab, B) over F7 has a similar effect as in the previous example.

We switch the focal point again for bar two and introduce a new scale. Now we're essentially ignoring the F chord and focusing on the overall D tonality of the tune. To keep ratcheting up the tension, the scale of choice here is D Melodic Minor (D, E, F, G, A, B, C#). It creates a strong dissonance against the F chord that is resolved in bar three.

Here's a useful scale pattern for the melodic minor scale.

D Melodic Minor scale pattern

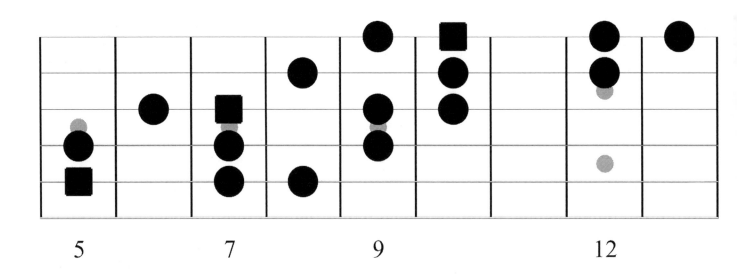

In bar four, we return to the D Harmonic Minor scale and the line is arranged in a classical manner that is reminiscent of the Baroque composers.

Example 4n

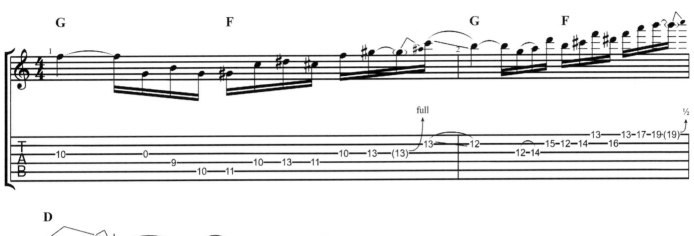

To continue building tension to the end of the solo, in the final section the D Harmonic Minor scale is also used over the A chord in bar one. This has a similar effect to playing it over the D dominant chord.

The D Harmonic Minor scale contains every chord tone of A7 (A, C#, E, G) plus brings the 11th (D), #5 (F) and b9 (Bb) color tones into the mix.

At the end of bar one, I added a passing F# note that doesn't belong to this scale but helped form the shape of the line, then on the first beat of bar two the A note is bent up a whole step to B, which is the 3rd of the G chord in that bar.

In bar three, I was thinking more about descending chromatically than using a specific scale, and had in mind the target note of the root of the A chord in bar four, which is played by bending the G note at the 20th fret up a whole step.

Example 4o

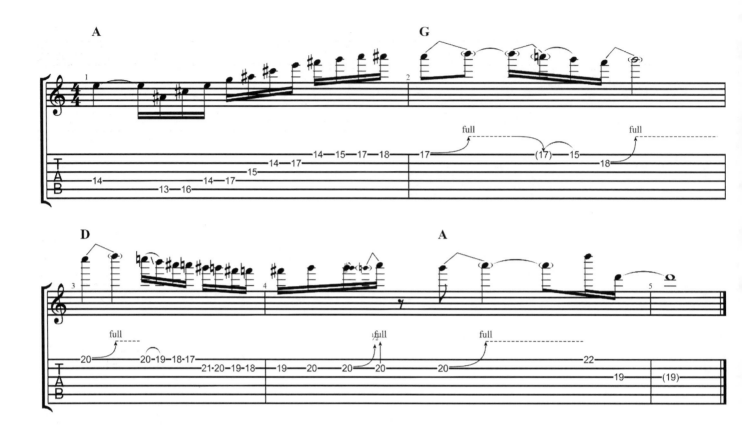

Now that you've practiced every section of the four solos, work at connecting them together to play the whole track.

Example 4p – Morse Code Blues

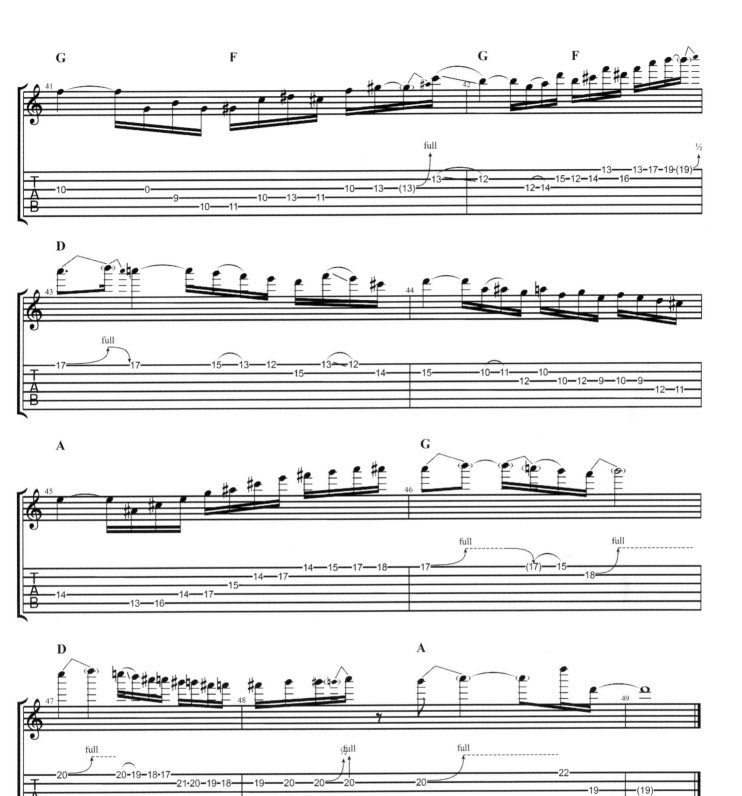

Conclusion

I hope you've enjoyed this study of melodic rock soloing. Guitar soloing is an art, and we have noted that all our favorite players tend to be great storytellers on the instrument – and that to become a storyteller with our instrument means working hard on our facility with phrasing.

In this book I've tried to pass on how I think when I set about creating guitar parts and solos. It's a compositional approach, because I believe that's the way to learn to play more melodically. Why not set yourself a challenge to use the backing tracks in this book to write your own melody parts, which then lead into your solos.

Make the melodies strong, catchy and memorable. As you begin to improvise and solo, remember to include the following phrasing devices we've used throughout this book:

- Employ question and answer phrases to achieve more vocal-like phrasing

- Use motifs i.e. short melodic ideas you can develop and build on

- Sequence your scale runs i.e. vary the note order, rather than playing scales straight up and down, and create patterns

- Add passing notes to familiar scale patterns e.g. adding chromatic notes to the familiar Mixolydian scale or major/minor pentatonic scales

- Create lines that skip strings to play wider, less predictable intervals

- Use rhythmic diversity to create interest and surprise in your playing

- Give your lines momentum and direction. In other words, have a target in mind and work towards it. Play lines that have a clear beginning, middle and end

- Last but not least, don't forget to use space. Not playing a note can be just as effective as playing one!

Good luck with your sonic explorations,

Steve.

Made in the USA
Middletown, DE
20 February 2024

50055403R00051